# Crafting Efficiency in Managerial Costing System Design

Pieter W. Buys

# Crafting Efficiency in Managerial Costing System Design

## An Integrated Design Science Approach

Pieter W. Buys🄳
Management Cybernetics Research
Entity
North-West University
Potchefstroom, South Africa

ISBN 978-981-97-0936-6        ISBN 978-981-97-0934-2   (eBook)
https://doi.org/10.1007/978-981-97-0934-2

This Palgrave Macmillan imprint is published by the registered company Springer Nature Singapore Pte Ltd.
The registered company address is: 152 Beach Road, #21-01/04 Gateway East, Singapore 189721, Singapore

Paper in this product is recyclable.

# FOREWORD

Design Science Research (DSR) is the research paradigm of choice for practice-inspired research that seeks to find novel solutions to challenging, sticky, wicked problems. In this endeavor, we recognize that it is a guided, emergent search through diagnosing the problem domain and building and evaluating possible solutions.

DSR evolved from the work of numerous scholars grounded in the information systems and technology domains. This occurred largely because of the rapid growth in and need for innovative, novel solutions to wicked problems facing practice during the rise of the information age. Researchers needed an approach—a paradigm—that went beyond theory building or theory testing. We needed an exploratory approach to research when the problem and solution domains were poorly understood and where the needed contribution to practitioner knowledge was as significant as that to academic knowledge. (Hevner et al. 2004) In these situations, we needed to begin the exploration of possible solutions without a clear understanding of what the final solution would be and often in the absence of theory to guide or explain the phenomenon at hand.

A key aspect of DSR was its grounding in the work of Nobel Prize Laureate Herbert A. Simon and his thoughts on design for "the artificial." He was one of a group of practitioners and scholars in the 1950s who recognized that some of the most interesting advances were set to occur in spaces that existed in the limitless expanse of the creativity of the human mind—not bounded by the physical constraints of natural laws. He and others recognized that nearly every human and organizational system and process, digital product, and service was ripe for transformation that increased utility and generated design knowledge for the next iteration or instantiation of the solution (Simon 1996).

Interestingly, although the science of the artificial—and thus DSR—originated in the information systems and technology domains, the opportunity for application of the DSR paradigm and research methods is nearly universal wherever there exists a system, process, product, or service that is not bounded by the physical. The reality is that nearly every business system and process is designed and exists "in the artificial." Innovation in accounting, finance, marketing, sales, and management systems and processes today is limited only by the imagination and creativity of the design team and driven by the rapidly evolving needs of our digital, virtual business, and social environment. Innovation in products and services inevitably requires a digital, virtual—aka artificial—component, even in the case of physical products. There isn't a business today that is not a digital business in one or more meaningful ways. In every case, DSR and DSR methods allow the researcher to co-create, co-build, and co-evaluate novel solutions that generate design knowledge and real solutions with an impact on the practitioner and the researcher.

Several methods exist to add rigor to the research process. The elaborated action design science research method (eADR) (Mullarkey and Hevner 2019) was developed from our experience in the conduct and evaluation of numerous DSR projects and "stands on the shoulders" of the original ADR work of Sein et al. (2011). The eADR research method provides the research–practitioner team with a map of the iterative design process, the rigorous build and evaluation of novel artifacts, and the path to sharing the new knowledge learned with academia and practice. With evidence offered in this volume, it turns out that these methods for the conduct of DSR translate very nicely and quite seamlessly across the business domains.

Over the last twenty years, we have seen the rise of the DSR research paradigm with broad application—and publication in the best academic and practitioner journals—across the IS and IT domains. (Gregor and Hevner 2013) In the last five years, we have been excited to see the "evangelization" and use of DSR to generate innovative solutions and wonderful design knowledge in the other practice-centered business domains. This volume offers those researchers examples to consider and approaches to exploit DSR and eADR in their research as they design for "the artificial" and generate novel solutions to sticky, wicked problems across the business systems, processes, products, and services landscape. I encourage you to use the research and examples in this volume to inspire you to join us in the journey to generate novel, necessary, and innovative solutions for the future of business.

Professor of Instruction
Director, Doctor of Business Administration (DBA) Program
Tampa General Hospital (TGH) Fellow
Extraordinary Professor, North-West University, Potchefstroom, South Africa
Fulbright Core Research Scholar
NSF Innovation I-Corps Fellow
Muma College of Business
School of Information Systems and Management
University of South Florida
Tampa, Florida

January 2024                                    Matthew Mullarkey, Ph.D.

## REFERENCES

Gregor, S. and Hevner, A.R. 2013. Positioning and presenting design science research for maximum impact. *MIS Quarterly*, 337–355.

Hevner, A.R., March, S.T., Park, J. and Ram, S. 2004. Design science in information systems research. *MIS Quarterly*, 28(1):75–115.

Mullarkey, M.T. and Hevner, A.R. 2019. An elaborated action design research process model. *European Journal of Information Systems*, 28(1):6–20.

Sein, M.K., Henfridsson, O., Purao, S., Rossi, M. and Lindgren, R. 2011. Action design research. *MIS Quarterly*, 37–56.

Simon, H.A. 1996. *The sciences of the artificial*. MIT Press.

# About This Book

This book has two main focuses: one is academic, concentrating on theoretical aspects like systems thinking, business process analysis, cost accounting, and scientific research and design. The other focus is industry-oriented, aiming to offer practical solutions for real management problems, particularly in effective managerial costing system design.

The importance of managerial costing in an organization's performance management is widely recognized, both in academic literature and within the manufacturing industry. However, many managerial costing systems are built on the misconception that they should align with financial reporting systems designed for external reporting, rather than being tailored to internal managerial needs. This misalignment is partly due to the complex nature of managerial costing, which involves various stakeholders, organizational systems, value chain functions, and diverse cost accounting techniques.

The book seeks to shed light on these complexities and demonstrate how an elaborate action design research approach, rooted in a design science paradigm, can effectively create robust managerial costing systems. This approach involves collaboration between academic researchers and industry practitioners and encompasses contextual iterative solution development activities, including problem formulation and refinement, solution design, and verification and validation of the proposed solution.

# CONTENTS

**1  Introduction**                                                          1
  *1.1  Background*                                                          1
  *1.2  Domain Contextualization*                                            2
       *1.2.1  Introduction*                                                 2
       *1.2.2  A Systems Approach to Cost Management*                        3
       *1.2.3  Business Process Relevance*                                   4
       *1.2.4  Purposeful Managerial Costing*                                5
       *1.2.5  Knowledge Deficit*                                            6
  *1.3  Problem Definition and Objective*                                    6
  *1.4  Research Method*                                                     8
       *1.4.1  Conceptual Paradigm*                                          8
       *1.4.2  Ethical Considerations*                                      11
  *1.5  Layout*                                                             12
  *1.6  In Conclusion*                                                      13
  *References*                                                              13

**2  A Design Science Methodology**                                        17
  *2.1  Background*                                                         17
  *2.2  Conceptual Design*                                                  18
  *2.3  Applied Method*                                                     19
       *2.3.1  Paradigmic Contextualisation*                                21
       *2.3.2  Conceptualizing Action Design Research*                      22
       *2.3.3  Elaborated Action Design Research Evolution*                 22
  *2.4  Research Team Composition*                                          27

2.4.1   *Introduction*                                                          27
2.4.2   *Industry Participants*                                                 27
2.4.3   *Knowledge Development*                                                 29
2.5   *In Conclusion*                                                           30
*References*                                                                    31

3   **Systems Thinking Foundation**                                            33
3.1   *Background*                                                              33
3.2   *Systems Theory*                                                         34
   3.2.1   *Systems Classification*                              34
   3.2.2   *Systems Fundamentals*                                35
   3.2.3   *System Design Framework*                             37
3.3   *Systems Engineering*                                                    40
   3.3.1   *Defining Systems Engineering*                        40
   3.3.2   *Application of Systems Engineering*                   41
   3.3.3   *Systems Engineering Methodology*                     42
3.4   *Cybernetics*                                                            43
   3.4.1   *Cybernetic Concept*                                  43
   3.4.2   *Cybernetic Principles*                               44
   3.4.3   *Management Cybernetics*                              46
   3.4.4   *Managerial Theories*                                 47
3.5   *In Conclusion*                                                          49
*References*                                                                   49

4   **Business Process Considerations**                                        53
4.1   *Background*                                                             53
4.2   *Definition of Business Process*                                        54
   4.2.1   *Business Process Modeling*                           54
   4.2.2   *Business Process Levels*                             55
   4.2.3   *Business Process Classification*                     57
   4.2.4   *Business Process Life Cycle*                         58
   4.2.5   *Business Process Improvement*                        60
4.3   *Business Process Management*                                           62
   4.3.1   *Business Process Reengineering*                      62
   4.3.2   *Model Abstraction*                                   63
4.4   *Business Process Modeling*                                             65
   4.4.1   *From the Value System to the Business Process*       65
   4.4.2   *Modeling Approaches*                                 66
4.5   *Chapter Summary*                                                       70
*References*                                                                   72

**5 Cost Accounting Perspectives** 77
5.1 *Background* 77
5.2 *Production Environment* 78
    5.2.1 *Job Costing* 78
    5.2.2 *Process Costing* 78
    5.2.3 *Operational Costing* 80
5.3 *Costing Concepts* 81
    5.3.1 *Cost Behavior* 81
    5.3.2 *Managerial Considerations* 84
5.4 *Cost Management* 85
    5.4.1 *Main Cost Centers: Production Department* 85
    5.4.2 *Secondary Cost Centers: Support Departments* 88
5.5 *Costing* 89
    5.5.1 *Approaches to Costing* 89
    5.5.2 *Methods of Costing* 90
5.6 *In Conclusion* 102
*References* 103

**6 First eADR Iteration: Problem Refinement** 107
6.1 *Guiding Principles for the Iteration of Diagnosis* 107
6.2 *Problem Formulation* 111
    6.2.1 *Framing the Problem* 111
    6.2.2 *Research Problem Corroboration* 112
6.3 *Building, Intervention, and Evaluation* 116
    6.3.1 *Systems Thinking Process Flow Model* 116
    6.3.2 *Business Processes Process Flow* 118
    6.3.3 *Cost Accounting Process Flow* 120
6.4 *Reflection and Learning* 122
6.5 *Formalization of Learning* 122
    6.5.1 *Systems Thinking Developmental Guide* 123
    6.5.2 *Business Processes Developmental Guide* 123
    6.5.3 *Cost Accounting Developmental Guide* 123
6.6 *In Conclusion* 123
*References* 129

**7 Second eADR Iteration: Solution Integration** 131
7.1 *Guiding Principles of the Design Iteration* 131
7.2 *Problem Formulation* 132
    7.2.1 *Problem Contextualization* 132
    7.2.2 *Dimensional Integration* 135

7.3   Building, Intervention, and Evaluation                          138
7.4   Reflection and Learning                                        138
7.5   Formalization of Learning                                      143
7.6   Chapter Summary                                                144
References                                                           145

8   Third eADR Iteration: Solution Validation                        147
8.1   Guiding Principles of the Implementation Iteration             147
8.2   Problem Formulation                                            151
8.3   Building, Intervention, and Evaluation                         153
      8.3.1   Verification of the Contextual System
              Environment Model                                      153
      8.3.2   Verification of the Developmental Guides                155
      8.3.3   Process Flow Verification                               156
8.4   Reflection and Learning                                        158
8.5   Formalization of Learning                                      167
8.6   Chapter Summary                                                168
References                                                           170

9   Summative Discussion                                             171
9.1   Introduction                                                   171
9.2   Reflection on Topic Actuality and Objectives                   172
9.3   Attainment of the Research Objective                           173
      9.3.1   Systems Thinking, Cost Accounting
              and Business Processes Intricacies                     173
      9.3.2   A Process Modeling Approach to Managerial
              Costing System Design                                  174
      9.3.3   Validating the Contextual Process Modeling
              Approach                                               175
9.4   Concluding Reflection                                          176
9.5   Final Thoughts                                                 177
References                                                           178

Index                                                                179

# ABOUT THE AUTHOR

**Pieter W. Buys** currently holds the position of Professor and Director of the *Applied Research in Management Cybernetics* research entity at North-West University, Potchefstroom, South Africa. With a blend of extensive academic expertise, corporate management, and consulting experience, he has assumed diverse leadership roles within these domains, spanning the manufacturing, engineering, information technology, and academic sectors in both Southern Africa and North America.

He is a Certified Management Accountant (CMA) from the Institute of Management Accountants based in the United States. His academic qualifications include advanced degrees in managerial accountancy, accounting philosophy, and engineering management. At the heart of his professional endeavors lies a dedicated research agenda, meticulously crafted to bridge the gap between academic inquiry in the broader management sciences and its practical relevance within organizational contexts. His research initiatives are purposefully geared toward making pragmatic contributions that have a tangible impact on businesses operating in the contemporary business environment, exemplifying dedication to advancing knowledge and fostering practical innovation within the field of management cybernetics.

# List of Figures

Fig. 1.1    Conceptual paradigm                                                    8
Fig. 1.2    Research method definition                                             9
Fig. 1.3    Stages in an elaborated action design research process
            (*Source* Adapted from Mullarkey and Hevner 2018)                     10
Fig. 2.1    Systems theory contextualization (*Source* Compiled
            from Kessler 2013; Pondy and Mitroff 1979)                            20
Fig. 2.2    Iterative elaborated action design research cycle (*Source*
            Adapted from Mullarkey and Hevner 2018)                               25
Fig. 2.3    Elaborated action design research iterations (*Source*
            Adapted from Mullarkey and Hevner 2018)                               26
Fig. 3.1    Conceptual systems environment                                        36
Fig. 3.2    Analysis level: managerial costing system design                      39
Fig. 3.3    Conceptual cybernetic feedback loop                                   45
Fig. 3.4    Systems-wide cybernetic feedback loops                                45
Fig. 4.1    Conceptual business process modeling                                  55
Fig. 4.2    Conceptual business process levels                                    56
Fig. 4.3    Business process hierarchy                                            58
Fig. 4.4    Conceptual business process life cycle                                59
Fig. 4.5    Primary abstraction dimensions                                        64
Fig. 4.6    Functional decomposition (*Source* Adapted from Porter
            1985)                                                                  66
Fig. 4.7    Illustration of a swimlane flowchart                                  68
Fig. 4.8    Illustration of a UML activity diagram                                69
Fig. 4.9    Illustration of a BPMN process model                                  71
Fig. 5.1    Cost flow overview: job costing                                       79

Fig. 5.2    Cost flow overview: process costing                                  80
Fig. 5.3    Fixed vs. variable cost behavior                                     82
Fig. 5.4    Holistic view of manufacturing-related costs                         86
Fig. 5.5    Direct costing versus absorption costing                             90
Fig. 5.6    Management of variances in direct costs                              92
Fig. 5.7    Management of variances in variable indirect costs                   93
Fig. 5.8    Management of variances in fixed indirect costs                      94
Fig. 5.9    Conceptual presentation of GPK's principles                          97
Fig. 5.10   Conceptual presentation of ABC's principles                          98
Fig. 5.11   Conceptual presentation of RCA's principles                         100
Fig. 6.1    Problem-centric eADR diagnosis iteration                            108
Fig. 6.2    Process flow of system thinking analysis                            117
Fig. 6.3    Process flow of business process analysis                           119
Fig. 6.4    Process flow of cost accounting analysis                            121
Fig. 7.1    Object-centric eADR design iteration                                132
Fig. 7.2    Conceptual integration                                              136
Fig. 7.3    Integrated process flow                                             139
Fig. 7.4    Contextual managerial costing environmental                         144
Fig. 8.1    Validation-centric eADR implementation iteration                    148
Fig. 8.2    Verified contextual managerial costing system
            environment model                                                   155
Fig. 8.3    Process flow for designing cost management systems                  163
Fig. 8.4    Verified and validated process model                                169

# LIST OF TABLES

| | | |
|---|---|---|
| Table 2.1 | Action design research methodology | 23 |
| Table 2.2 | Research team composition | 28 |
| Table 6.1 | Diagnosis activities | 109 |
| Table 6.2 | Developmental guide: systems theory | 124 |
| Table 6.3 | Developmental guide: systems engineering | 125 |
| Table 6.4 | Developmental guide: cybernetics | 126 |
| Table 6.5 | Developmental guide: business process definition | 127 |
| Table 6.6 | Developmental guide: business process management | 127 |
| Table 6.7 | Developmental guide: business process modeling | 128 |
| Table 6.8 | Developmental guide: cost accounting environment | 128 |
| Table 6.9 | Developmental guide: costing concepts | 128 |
| Table 6.10 | Developmental guide: cost accounting | 129 |
| Table 7.1 | Design activities | 133 |
| Table 7.2 | Multilevel dimensional costing process analysis | 140 |
| Table 8.1 | Implementation activities | 149 |
| Table 8.2 | First verification design statement | 152 |
| Table 8.3 | First validation design statement | 153 |
| Table 8.4 | Second verification design statement | 154 |
| Table 8.5 | Third verification design statement | 156 |
| Table 8.6 | Systems thinking developmental guide | 157 |
| Table 8.7 | Systems thinking supporting notes | 158 |
| Table 8.8 | Cost accounting developmental guide | 159 |
| Table 8.9 | Cost accounting supporting notes | 160 |
| Table 8.10 | Business process developmental guide | 161 |
| Table 8.11 | Business process supplementary notes | 162 |

Table 8.12    Fourth verification design statement                                        162
Table 8.13    Verified multilevel dimensional costing process analysis        164
Table 8.14    Fifth verification design statement                                         167
Table 8.15    Second validation design statement                                      168

# CHAPTER 1

# Introduction

## 1.1 Background

Contrary to the predictions made by doomsayers in the 1980s (Peavy 1990), actual results indicate that the manufacturing sectors of many countries remained significant and maintained regular contributions to their respective gross domestic product (GDP) (UNIDO 2018). This suggests that manufacturing continues to play a critical role in global economic prosperity. The contemporary industrial complex is in the midst of the *Fourth Industrial Revolution*, characterized by real-time collaboration between humans, technologies, and systems to address social issues (Mohelska and Sokolova 2018). This revolution integrates industrial processes that have far-reaching implications for manufacturing (Griffiths and Ooi 2018). Successful manufacturing organizations share a common trait: A highly agile environment characterized by continual innovation and change that lead to cutting-edge product offerings. This agility, however, influences business processes and cost management. To achieve value creation and economic viability goals, organizations must systematically understand their internal and external operational contexts and comprehend their cost structures to allocate and manage resources effectively (Raef et al. 2019a). This poses a conundrum: The designing of effective managerial costing systems in a complex and volatile business environment.

© The Author(s), under exclusive license to Springer Nature Singapore Pte Ltd. 2024
P. W. Buys, *Crafting Efficiency in Managerial Costing System Design*,
https://doi.org/10.1007/978-981-97-0934-2_1

This book acknowledges the significance of effective cost management in the current technologically dynamic manufacturing environment and elucidates how a design science-based research approach may enable the design of effective managerial costing systems.

## 1.2    DOMAIN CONTEXTUALIZATION

### *1.2.1    Introduction*

When the steps of our forebears are retraced to gain some understanding of the roots of cost management, we should linger on Luca Pacioli—a fifteenth-century Italian friar. He is still widely regarded as a highly influential mathematician of his time (Montebelli 2015) and is often credited as the "father of accounting" (Cluskey et al. 2007). In his mathematical compendium published in 1494, titled "*Summa de Arithmetica Geometria Proportioni et Proportionalita*", 27 pages are dedicated to bookkeeping, specifically the section, "*Particularis de Computis et Scripturis*" (Sangster et al. 2008). In this specific section, he explains the accounting practices of that era (Montebelli 2015), and covers various aspects of cost and management accounting, including budgeting and variance analyses (Rashid 2016). During that period, accounting skills were primarily associated with merchants who received their education in vernacular schools where practical problem-solving and business-related knowledge, known as Abaco, was taught (Montebelli 2015; Sangster et al. 2008).

During the *First Industrial Revolution*, as noted by Johnson and Kaplan (1987) and Solomons (1994), much of the early work in cost accounting was published by engineers rather than accountants, highlighting the *practice-based* origins of the cost management discipline. Examples hereof include:

- H. Metcalf's "*Cost of Manufacture*" (1885).
- E. Garcke and J. Manger's "*Factory Accounts: Their Principles and Practice*" (1887).
- J. Mann's "*Cost Records or Factory Accounting*" (1903) and "*On Cost or Expense*" (1904).
- J.L. Nicholson's "*Factory Organization and Costs*" (1909).

Contemporary literature, including Appelbaum et al. (2017), Askarany and Smith (2008), Cardoş and Pete (2011), Chea (2011), Johnson and Kaplan (1987), Tsai et al. (2015), and Van der Stede (2017), emphasize the importance of effective cost management. In light of all the above, it is evident that effective cost management is acknowledged as an integral management function in a practical business context.

Nevertheless, consensus on its application is still needed. For instance, proper cost knowledge is crucial in lean manufacturing environments with Chick (2016) highlighting the need for a comprehensive understanding of product costs. In contrast, Cokins (2001) suggests that the lean community often finds cost accounting systems too complex. These diverse outlooks, but perhaps in a sense supplemental as well, justify the validation that conventional approaches to cost management may not provide sufficient managerial costing information for practical management decision support.

### 1.2.2 A Systems Approach to Cost Management

According to Potts et al. (2020), contemporary organizations face the challenge of engineering complex systems to meet the demands of an interconnected world. Kessler (2013) adds another dimension by defining the organization as a system—a distinct unit composed of interconnected and interacting components. Against this background, the value of adopting a systems perspective in organizational cost management is evident in its integration with performance management initiatives and its application within the managerial costing system. Raef et al. (2019a) concur when stating that value is found in adopting a systems approach when designing managerial costing systems: It allows for an integrated design approach. Collopy (2019) believes that design thinking is increasingly recognized as an integrative management concept. However, when faced with a complex design task, such as designing a managerial costing system, a single design cycle would likely fulfill only some of the requirements. Instead, an iterative guided emergent process may be needed in which multiple stakeholders and operational functions are engaged to design and validate various artifact iterations.

In this context, systems theory suggests that systems share common characteristics across scientific disciplines and implies that cross-disciplinary thinking and interdependent processes exist in contemporary society, including organizations and their management activities. Kessler (2013) emphasizes the law of unintended consequences within systems theory, and highlights how developments in one part of a system could lead to unexpected and potentially undesired outcomes in other parts of the system. In the context of cost information in management accounting practice, the prevalence of information distortion may be attributed to the *system* in which the cost information is conceptualized and generated. Systems thinking expands the scope of cost accounting by integrating cost management with strategic initiatives, such as organizational planning, control, and customer management (Chick 2016). In doing so it also contributes to organizational supply and value chain optimization that allows for an analysis of cost driver information and the identification of opportunities for improvement in other operational areas.

### 1.2.3   Business Process Relevance

In support of the above, Bhaskar (2018) states that organizations comprise multiple business processes, which are collections of sub-processes aimed at generating output. Therefore, effective business process management should lead to higher performance levels and managerial effectiveness. Core processes, such as product/service development, order generation, order fulfillment, and customer services, form the foundation of most organizations. These core processes revolve around customer-centricity, and the sub-processes within cost accounting support the approach of placing customers at the center of all decisions and strategies.

When business processes are analyzed and evaluated, it is necessary to unpack the core processes systematically to achieve an integrated understanding, which involves process modeling. Process model types are categorized into *descriptive models* that describe existing processes, *prescriptive models* that define desired processes and their execution, and *explanatory models* that clarify the rationale of specific processes. This understanding is supported by Kuokkanen (2022), who asserts that process modeling involves classifying similar processes into a model that describes or prescribes how processes should be conducted. Additional support is provided by Bronzo et al. (2013), who discovered that when business processes are individually analyzed, it often positively

impacts organizational performance. Consequently, organizations prioritizing effective business process management should focus on improving
their capacity to integrate data flow, known as process intelligence,
and gain a deeper understanding of the financial and cost implications,
referred to as financial intelligence.

### 1.2.4  Purposeful Managerial Costing

Cost accounting involves determining the cost of an object and ensuring
effective and sustainable utilization of available resources. High-quality
products at competitive prices are essential for long-term value creation
and financial viability and require a genuine understanding of cost drivers.
As manufacturing evolved through the various industrial revolutions,
customized products replaced mass-produced ones, leading to increased
indirect costs in engineering, logistics, quality control, setup, marketing,
and sales. Bearing this in mind, White and Clinton (2014) are of the
opinion that non-conventional cost management approaches recognize
the importance of analyzing business processes to generate relevant cost
information.

Managerial costing primarily aims to provide future-oriented management information, while financial accounting summarizes historical financial data (Raef et al. 2019b). However, a reliance on externally focused
financial information for internal management decisions creates a discon-
nect with the internal focus of the management accounting discipline.
This reliance on externally orientated systems contradicts the objective of
managerial costing to associate financial information accurately with the
dynamic realities of an organization's operating context.

Aligning managerial costing systems with business processes could
provide relatable management information for short-term operational
and long-term strategic decisions that contribute to organizational value
creation and viability (James 2013; Rundora et al. 2013). When the relationship between product offerings and associated resources is considered,
cost management approaches that account for operational activities could
effectively measure organizational process effectiveness and performance.
A survey by Stratton et al. (2009) demonstrated that cost management approaches grounded in operational realities provide substantial
value-added benefits. These benefits include consistently applying relevant
cost accounting techniques, improved accuracy in cost allocations, and

enhanced support for management decision-making. Relevant cost information becomes indispensable for the management functions of planning, measuring, analyzing, and controlling organizational and operational performance, hence *managerial costing*.

### 1.2.5    Knowledge Deficit

Based on the above, we acknowledge that the business problem of effective cost management is *wicked*, i.e., difficult to solve because of its complex and interconnected nature. As a function, managerial costing must arguably be viewed as integral to a broader organizational system. It is, therefore, essential to understand that it goes beyond mere accounting, and is influenced by an organization's external value stream and its internal operations. Given the diverse methods, objectives, and functions within cost accounting, it is crucial to identify and select quite diligently the most suitable cost accounting methods and approaches to be incorporated into the managerial costing system.

This book aims to bridge the knowledge deficit between the intended purpose of managerial costing information, which is to support contextual business decision-making, and how the system that generates the information should be designed and ultimately to provide relevant and applicable management insights. The significance of bridging this knowledge gap is highlighted by the efforts of leading professional accounting bodies, such as the Institute of Management Accountants, who consider the issue in publications, such as "*The conceptual framework for managerial costing*" (White and Clinton 2014).

## 1.3    Problem Definition and Objective

Historically, manufacturing organizations relied heavily on labor and less on the application of sophisticated technologies. More recently, the influence of advanced technologies has grown significantly across all operations. Traditionally, indirect costs constituted a small proportion of the overall manufacturing costs and were allocated based on (direct) labor hours due to their causal relationship. However, with technological advancements labor hours decreased and indirect costs increased (proportionally), leading to a mismatch in allocation, while modern management philosophies like lean manufacturing and total quality management emphasize the importance of strategic managerial costing efforts. Conventional cost management approaches are criticized for generating information that is not robust enough for sound decision-making. These 'restrictions' could be attributed to the divergent purposes of the financial and management accounting disciplines, which focus respectively on externally and internally orientated management perspectives.

Despite the numerous costing approaches and methods available, the fundamental goal of all managerial costing systems remains unchanged: To provide accurate estimates of resource consumption to support organizational and managerial objectives. We contend that effective managerial costing systems should consider the specific organizational context, employ appropriate cost accounting techniques, and generate pertinent management information for decision-making. Our assertion highlights the problem, which questions how an adequate and contextually relevant managerial costing system could be designed to accommodate distinct operational characteristics, stakeholder dynamics, and influences unique to each organization.

In the context of effective organizational management, adopting a systems approach offers a reliable framework for designing complex systems across various domains. It provides a formal method for addressing the above-stated problem. Therefore, this book's main objective is to illustrate a systems-based design science approach to *develop effective managerial costing systems*. This approach would result in creating an integrated process model (hereafter referred to as the 'model') able to guide the design of effective managerial costing systems.

To reach this objective, the attainment of three sub-objectives becomes essential: (i) to understand the relationship between business processes and cost accounting within systems thinking frameworks; (ii) to develop supporting building blocks to design a managerial costing system that considers organizational systems and operational complexities; and (iii) to validate these building blocks in context. While the development process explained within this book may primarily focus on the manufacturing industry, the ultimate design approach (or process model) could be applicable as a universal framework for developing managerial costing systems across multiple industries.

## 1.4    Research Method

### 1.4.1    Conceptual Paradigm

The research paradigm sets the context for linking a project's theoretical foundation to its practical implications. Figure 1.1 illustrates the interaction between theoretical and practical environments within a design science paradigm (framework), and showcases how these interactions could guide the development of a practical solution, as follows:

- Firstly, the design science paradigm applies academic principles to solve real-life business problems by fostering iterative interactions between industry and academia to develop optimal solutions.
- Secondly, the practical objective is to develop a systems-based model to guide the design of managerial costing systems that takes into account the realities of modern manufacturing.

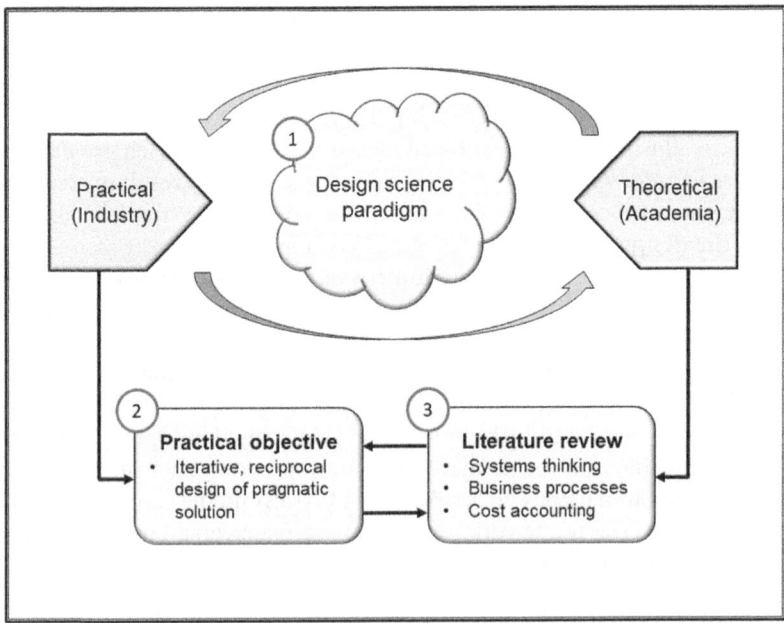

**Fig. 1.1**    Conceptual paradigm

- Thirdly, the theoretical context encompasses a literature review that establishes a firm foundation for the subsequent process model by incorporating systems thinking, business processes, and cost accounting.

In the context of the above-illustrated paradigm, the stated book objective and sub-objectives would be achieved by aligning with the proposed three pillars concept, as illustrated in Fig. 1.2.

In *Phase I*, the model's foundation is developed based on a comprehensive literature review that enhances the understanding of current academic and industry realities, essential for developing an effective managerial costing system. The first sub-objective is partially achieved through a literature review of systems thinking, business processes, and cost accounting (to be covered in Chapters 3–5), which elucidate the complexities associated with these pillars. Systems thinking provides insights into contextualizing organizations within a systems theory framework; business processes emphasize its direct impact on effective cost management practices; and cost accounting encompasses its various dimensions, approaches, and methods.

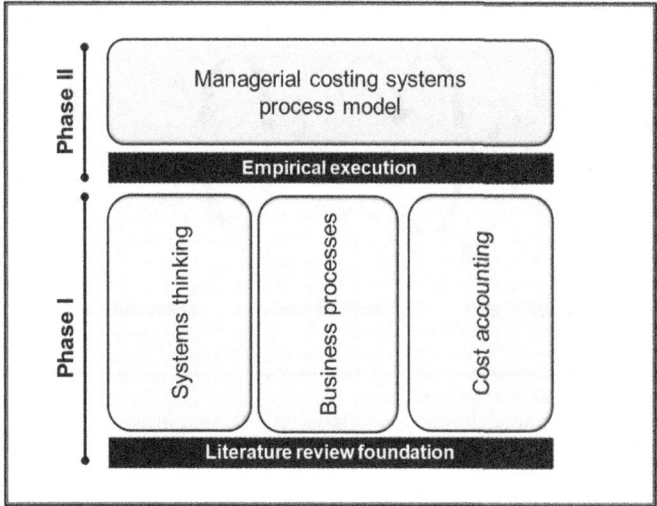

**Fig. 1.2**   Research method definition

In *Phase II*, the empirical execution adopts an *elaborated action design research*[1] approach, which involves collaboration within a researcher-practitioner team to define and develop innovative solutions for the identified problem. This approach follows a series of iterations, including a problem-centric diagnosis stage, followed by object-centric design, validation-centric implementation, and observation-centric evolution stages, as conceptualized by Mullarkey and Hevner (2018) (refer to Fig. 1.3):

The empirical research context in this book follows the first three iterations: Problem-centric, object-centric, and validation-centric iterations, as shown in the illustration above. In reaching the book's main objective, the process supports the following activities:

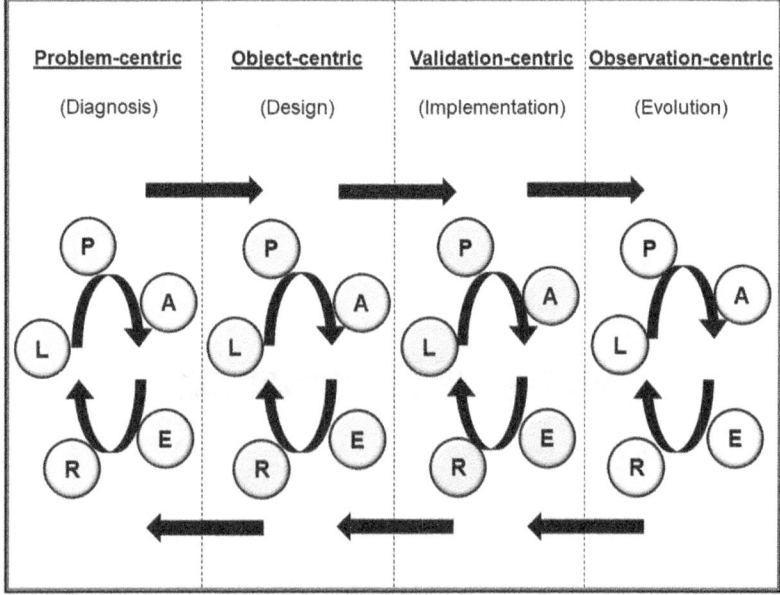

**Fig. 1.3**  Stages in an elaborated action design research process (*Source* Adapted from Mullarkey and Hevner 2018)

---

[1] Detailed discussion in Chapter Two.

- In supplementing the literature review, the *problem-centric diagnosis* iteration refines and validates the research problem that leads to context-specific developmental artifacts per the proposed three-pillar approach.
- The subsequent *object-centric design* iteration focuses on integrating the three pillars into an integrated process flow and contextual (managerial costing) systems environment.
- The final *validation-centric implementation* iteration oversees the verification and validation of the developmental artifacts per the previous iterations.

During the execution of these iterations, a researcher-practitioner team would include senior industry experts with comprehensive knowledge of the manufacturing industry's demands and challenges. In doing so, the design process entails an iterative and reciprocal design process, with the intended result being an industry-applicable solution. These iterations are unpacked in Chapters 6–8.

### *1.4.2   Ethical Considerations*

Ethics is a key component of academic and business research, as highlighted by Ciulla et al. (2017) and Tseng et al. (2010). The significance of ethical considerations cannot be overemphasized, especially when research involves human (or animal) participants. It is crucial to prioritize human dignity and ensure ethical treatment throughout the data collection process. The project, upon which this book is based, adhered to the appropriate ethical research guidelines and acquired the necessary institutional ethical approvals.

The industry participants involved in this project were chosen based on their relevant industry experience. Their participation was voluntary, and they provided written consent. Personal or company-specific information was not collected, and the participants were able to withdraw from the project at any given time. The collected data focus solely on business-related details that support the book's objectives and were based on the participants' industry experience, expertise, and opinions. The gathered information and knowledge were used conceptually to inform the design and development of a comprehensive model.

## 1.5   Layout

The layout of the book focuses on the aforementioned objectives and includes the following chapters:

- This chapter introduces the background and topic relevance by highlighting the interconnectedness of systems thinking, business process analyses, and cost accounting in modern manufacturing. The book's objectives and significance are also outlined to support the topic's relevance.
- Chapter 2 presents the methodology, and explains the application of the design science-based research approach within a systems theory framework. Additionally, the chapter addresses methodological rigor considerations to ensure the envisaged model's validity.
- Chapter 3 focuses on systems thinking and its relevance in context. It explores three meaningful subject contexts: systems theory, systems engineering, and management cybernetics. This chapter provides the foundational knowledge of systems thinking necessary for developing the envisaged model in a research context.
- Chapter 4 emphasizes the significance of a business process analysis. It pinpoints the importance of a business process and value stream analysis in designing a high-quality managerial costing system. This chapter provides the necessary foundational knowledge of business processes for developing the model in context.
- Chapter 5, the final literature-centric chapter, centers on cost accounting and its complexities. It delves into important costing concepts related to cost management, costing systems, costing methods, and approaches. This chapter provides the necessary foundational cost accounting knowledge to develop the model.
- Chapter 6 targets the problem-centric diagnosis iteration of the research process that involves a researcher-practitioner team that includes industry experts. The objectives include understanding, defining, and validating the experienced business problem under consideration and developing (diagnostic) process flow models.
- Chapter 7 concentrates on the object-centric design iteration of the research process by involving industry experts as part of the researcher-practitioner team. The focus is on refining the first iteration process flow model from a managerial perspective through continued engagement with industry experts.

- Chapter 8 aims to validate the developed artifact, i.e., the model, during the implementation iteration. A second set of industry participants experienced in designing and implementing managerial costing systems forms part of the researcher-practitioner team for this iteration.
- The conclusive Chapter 9 provides a discussion and summary of the project's achievements with regard to the research objective and sub-objectives. It also includes recommendations and highlights opportunities for future research in the field.

## 1.6   In Conclusion

This chapter offered contextual information about and justification for the book, including an overview of the theoretical disciplines, research problem, objectives, and a literature overview of a business process analysis and cost management concepts. It was noted that the book's focus is on an illustration of how a design science-based approach in collaboration with a researcher-practitioner team could be used to develop an integrated process model (or approach) to support the design of effective managerial costing systems. The next chapter provides a detailed unpacking of the underlying design science-based approach employed in this book.

### References

Appelbaum, D., Kogan, A., Vasarhelyi, M. and Yan, Z. 2017. Impact of business analytics and enterprise systems on managerial accounting. *International Journal of Accounting Information Systems*, 25:29–44.

Askarany, D. and Smith, M. 2008. Diffusion of innovation and business size: A longitudinal study of PACIA. *Managerial Auditing Journal*, 23(9):900–916.

Bhaskar, H.L. 2018. Business process reengineering: A process based management tool. *Serbian Journal of Management*, 13(1):63–87.

Bronzo, M., de Resende, P.T.V., de Oliviera, M.P.V., McCormack, K.P., de Sousa, P.R. and Ferreira, R.L. 2013. Improving performance aligning business analytics with process orientation. *International Journal of Information Management*, 33:300–307.

Cardoş, I.R. and Pete, Ş. 2011. Activity-based costing (ABC) and Activity-based management (ABM) implementation: Is this the solution for organizations to gain profitability? *Romanian Journal of Economics*, 32(1):151–168.

Chea, A.C. 2011. Activity-based costing systems in the service sector: A strategic approach for enhancing managerial decision making and competitiveness. *International Journal of Business and Management*, 6(11):3–10.

Chick, G. 2016. *Strategic cost management: Lean production at a global vehicle manufacturer*. Series: Kogan Page Case Study Library. [London]: Kogan Page. 2016. eBook.

Ciulla, J.B., Knights, D., Mabey, C. and Tomkins, L. 2017. Philosophical contributions to leadership ethics. *Business Ethics Quarterly*, 28(1):1–14.

Cluskey, G.R., Ehlen, C.R. and Rivers, R. 2007. Accounting theory: Missing in action. *Management Accounting Quarterly*, 8(2):24–31, Winter.

Collopy, F. 2019. Why the failure of systems thinking should inform the future of design thinking. *Design Issues*, 35(2):97–100.

Cokins, G. 2001. *Activity-based cost management: An executive's guide*. New York: Wiley.

Griffiths, F. and Ooi, M. 2018. The Fourth Industrial Revolution—Industry 4.0 and IoT. *IEEE Instrumentation & Measurement Magazine*, 21(6):29–43.

James, P.C. 2013. An analysis of the factors influencing the adoption of activity-based costing (ABC) in the financial sector in Jamaica. *International Journal of Business and Social Research*, 3(7):8–18.

Johnson, H.T. and Kaplan, R.S. 1987. *Relevance lost: The rise and fall of management accounting*. Boston: Harvard Business School Press.

Kessler, E.H. (ed.). 2013. *Encyclopedia of management theory*. Sage reference, Pace University.

Kuokkanen, J. 2022. Vertical-horizontal distinction in resolving the abstraction, hierarchy, and generality problems of the mechanistic account of physical computation. *Synthese*, 200:247. https://doi.org/10.1007/s11229-022-03725-8.

Mohelska, H. and Sokolova, M. 2018. Management approaches for Industry 4.0—The organizational culture perspective. *Technological & Economic Development of Economy*, 24(6):2225–2240.

Montebelli, V. 2015. Luca Pacioli and perspective (part I). *Lettera Matematica*, 3:135–141. https://doi.org/10.1007/s40329-015-0090-4.

Mullarkey, M. and Hevner, A. 2018. An elaborated action design research process model. *European Journal of Information Systems*, 28(1):6–20.

Peavy, D.E. 1990. It's time for change. *Management Accounting*, 71(8):31–35.

Potts, M.W., Sartor, P.A., Johnson, A. and Bullock, S. 2020. Assaying the importance of system complexity for the systems engineering community. *Systems Engineering*, 23:579–596.

Raef, R., Cokins, G., Hicks, D., Krumwiede, K., Swain, M. and White, L. 2019a. *Developing an effective managerial cost model*. Statements on Management Accounting. Institute of Management Accountants (IMA), Montvale: N.J.

Raef, R., Cokins, G., Hicks, D., Krumwiede, K., Swain, M. and White, L. 2019b. *Costing system attributes that support good decision making*. Statements on Management Accounting. Institute of Management Accountants (IMA), Montvale: N.J.

Rashid, M. 2016. Standard costing practices in listed pharmaceutical industries in Bangladesh. *The Cost and Management*, 44(6):44–50.

Rundora, R., Ziemerink, T. and Oberholzer, M. 2013. Activity-based costing in small manufacturing firms: South African study. *Journal of Applied Business Research*, 29(2):485–498.

Sangster, A., Stoner, G.N. and McCarthy, P. 2008. The market for Luca Pacioli's Summa Arithmetica. *Accounting Historians Journal*, 35(1):111–134, June.

Solomons, D. 1994. Retrospective: Costing pioneers: Some links with the past. *The Accounting Historians Journal*, 21(2):135–149.

Stratton, W.O., Desroches, D., Lawson, R.A. and Hatch, T. 2009. Activity-based costing: Is it still relevant? *Management Accounting Quarterly*, 10(3):31–40.

Tsai, W.H., Tsaur, T., Chou, Y., Liu, J., Hsu, J. and Hsieh, C. 2015. Integrating the activity-based costing system and life-cycle assessment into green decision-making. *International Journal of Production Research*, 53(2):451–465.

Tseng, H., Duan, C., Tung, H. and Kung, H. 2010. Modern business ethics research: Concepts, theories, and relationships. *Journal of Business Ethics*, 91(4):587–597.

UNIDO (United Nations Industrial Development Organisation). 2018. Industrial Development Report 2018. Demand for manufacturing: Driving inclusive and sustainable industrial development (ISBN978–92–1–106445–1). Vienna.

Van der Stede, W.A. 2017. "Global" management accounting research: Some reflections. *Journal of International Accounting Research*, 16(2):1–8.

White, L.R. and Clinton, B.D. 2014. *The conceptual framework for managerial costing*. Institute of Management Accountants (IMA), Montvale: N.J.

# CHAPTER 2

# A Design Science Methodology

The previous chapter provided an introductory overview of the book's objective and the topic under consideration. This chapter explains the foundational approach followed in our endeavors to develop a design methodology (i.e., the *integrated* model), to enable effective managerial costing systems design.

## 2.1 BACKGROUND

Contemporary manufacturing organizations are acknowledged as complex environments with diverse processes and objectives. These environments involve intricate systems encompassing people, structures, and technologies. Consequently, research in this domain is expected to be complex. Business research is a systematic investigation to generate information that addresses managerial problems. While acknowledging the perceived gap between research and practice, Sein et al. (**2011**) emphasize that *business research* should have dual objectives: Making theoretical contributions and solving practical business problems. Building on our assertion that an integrated three-pillar model could guide the design of effective managerial costing systems, this chapter outlines the approach that was followed.

It is crucial to clarify the approach followed, since the *design science paradigm* in which our managerial costing systems design model was

P. W. Buys, *Crafting Efficiency in Managerial Costing System Design*,
https://doi.org/10.1007/978-981-97-0934-2_2

developed is of central importance. In the scientific justification thereof, a conceptual research design establishes the data collection, measurement, and analysis framework. In contrast, the research method applied explains the techniques used to gather data and present findings. While interconnected, the *design* aspect directs the comprehensive foundational perspective of the undertaking, and the *methods* aspect focuses on the specific processes and tools used.

## 2.2   Conceptual Design

We justify the approach followed on the following philosophical and theoretical foundations. In terms of our philosophical grounding, we considered two related aspects:

- Epistemology: Taken as the theory of knowledge generation, epistemology in this context refers to the scientific framework in which we conducted our research. In accordance with Mouton's (2011) *Three Worlds* framework, we distinguish between *World I* as related to knowledge used for daily tasks; *World II*, which involves scientific knowledge used for research; and *World III*, which focuses on the philosophy of science and justifications for actions. In a managerial costing system design, the system is considered part of the physical reality, while requirements and design specifications belong to the realm of abstract knowledge. As such, this book applies conceptual and scientific knowledge to analyze a business problem by creating an artifact (solution) applicable to a real-world context. Abstract knowledge is, therefore, bridged with scientific knowledge to address physical realities.
- Methodology: Three frameworks are proposed within the methodological paradigm (Kivunja and Kuyini 2017) namely, the *positivistic*, which emphasizes empiricism and verification; the *critical*, which involves deconstructing the world; and the *interpretivistic*, which focuses on understanding and interpreting research findings. The essence of using a design science-based approach to the problem of managerial costing systems design is found in the interpretivistic framework when gained knowledge is utilized to develop and validate the model to be used when designing managerial costing systems.

With regard to our theoretical grounding, we align with Kessler's (2013) categorization of contemporary organizational theories within a systems theory (paradigm), and we emphasize the notion of an *organizational unit of inquiry* with interconnected and interacting parts. As indicated in the contextualization found in Fig. 2.1, various (management) theories differ in their distinct motivations and processes:

As illustrated, within an (organizational) systems theory framework, managerial costing systems could be justified within (i) rational systems theories with a focus on organizational goals; (ii) natural systems theories with a focus on interdepartmental goals; and (iii) open systems theories with a focus on the organization's relationships with its external environment. Developing a managerial costing system, which plays a crucial role within an organization and extends to the broader external environment, requires, therefore, an acknowledgment of interdependence.

Finally, our approach could be classified as descriptive where the focus was on the problem of effective cost management with an exploratory element, as the form and function of the model still needed to be discovered. The level was considered to be applied research, as it aimed to solve the cost management problem by making use of a qualitative approach in data collection and data analysis during the design of the model. Given the project objectives, our inductive reasoning approach aimed to generate new academic knowledge, while also contributing to industry knowledge.

## 2.3   APPLIED METHOD

The method that was followed included literary and empirical components to achieve the book's objectives. Firstly, the aim of the literature foundation (Chapters Three to Five) was to establish a foundation of the three pillars: Systems thinking; business processes; and cost accounting. This involved conducting a systematic review of published literature from academic journals and conference proceedings; and analyzing textbooks, subject-specific periodicals, and reports to provide a literary contextualization of these pillars. Secondly, the empirical aspects built on the above-mentioned aim to address the business management problem of ineffective managerial costing systems. As such, the method fell within a framework of two problem-solving classes: Purely technical business problems and socio-technical business problems. Iivari and Venable (2009) identified design science and action research as the corresponding paradigms for these problem classes.

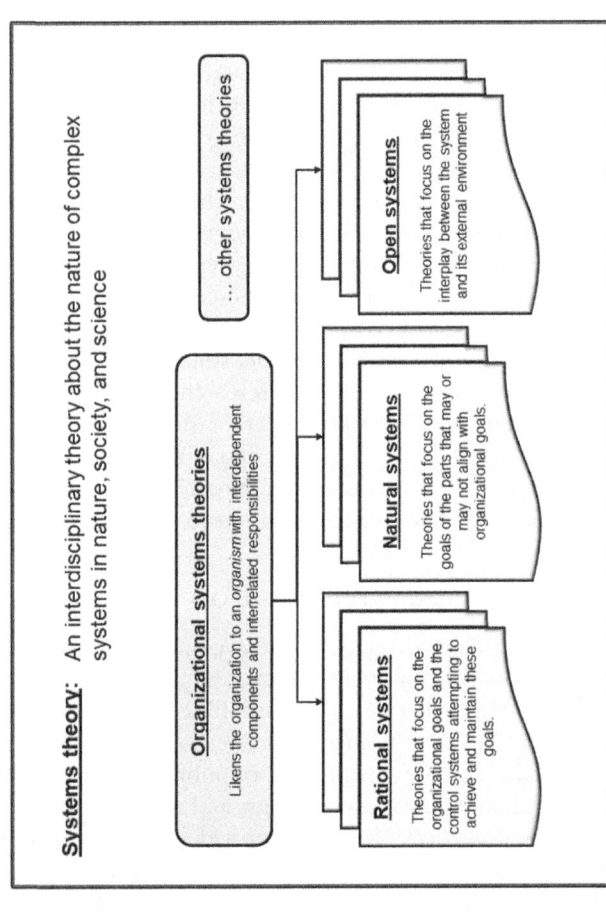

**Fig. 2.1** Systems theory contextualization (*Source* Compiled from Kessler 2013; Pondy and Mitroff 1979)

### 2.3.1   Paradigmic Contextualisation

All research aims to expand knowledge by identifying gaps, and confirming, or developing new knowledge. This book primarily focuses on developing new knowledge, which justified a design science paradigm, as explained below:

- Design science research (DSR) has been implicitly practiced by engineers for centuries. It focuses on creating innovative practices, capabilities, and products/services by addressing technical problems and innovations (Sein et al. 2011). As a methodology, DSR aims to develop prescriptive design knowledge by creating artifacts that solve specific problems. The iterative process of DSR involves shifting between the design process and the design artifact by supporting practical problem-solving objectives. DSR is centered around building and evaluating artifacts that contribute to practical concerns.
- Action research (AR) is a data-based problem-solving approach that originates from scientific investigation. In contrast to traditional scientific research, which focuses on studying problems, AR aims to study the issue and develop interventions to solve it (Ebersön et al. 2021). It addresses socio-technical problems and innovations by exploring organizational and human phenomena through the investigation, design, implementation, management, and use of systems, frameworks, and models. AR contributes to the development and validation of management theories.

While AR approaches are characterized by problem-solving techniques based on theoretical foundations, DSR approaches employ an engineering perspective, and aim to address general unsituated problems by creating new realities through the development of artifacts. The absence of an effective managerial costing system is not isolated but indicative of a specific problem as well as a broader class of problems. In the context of this book, the development of a managerial costing systems design model, therefore, aligned with the objectives of both DSR and AR.

### 2.3.2   Conceptualizing Action Design Research

While some scholars argue that DSR and AR approaches are essentially the same (Järvinen 2007), others maintain that they are quite distinct (Iivari and Venable 2009). Nevertheless, the discussion surrounding their similarities and differences suggests a potential evolution in the design sciences methodology, arguably leading to the emergence of action design research (ADR).

ADR aims to generate prescriptive design knowledge by developing and evaluating artifacts in organizational settings (Petersson and Lundberg 2016; Ward et al. 2023). Cronholm and Göbel (2019) opine that it emphasizes intervention and has been found to have solid theoretical foundations. Sein et al. (2011) propose four stages in the ADR methodology: Problem formulation; building, intervention, and evaluation (BIE); reflection and learning; and formalization of learning. These stages incorporate seven ADR principles, outlined in Table 2.1.

An ADR approach to business research combines elements of addressing a specific business issue with a tested solution, and incorporates reflection and learning. The stages and principles described in the table established the research foundation for designing and validating our proposed model.

### 2.3.3   Elaborated Action Design Research Evolution

To tackle the issue of not only realizing the presence and reality of a problem, but also vital to grasp its essence, a *researcher-practitioner* team engaged in delving into the underlying phenomenon. In doing so, knowledge of the problem domain was developed. In an attempt to address the issue of solving complex and intractable problems, Mullarkey and Hevner (2018) proposed certain areas of elaboration within the application of ADR. Their first proposal is that the elaborated action design research (eADR) process should include the problem definition (P), artifact creation (A), evaluation (E), reflection (R), and learning (L) activities (depicted in Fig. 2.2):

As illustrated, the eADR approach allows for multiple iterations to ensure a proper understanding of the problem in its context. A second suggestion identifies specific focused stages (iterations) in the overall design process as follows (see Fig. 2.3):

**Table 2.1** Action design research methodology

*Stages and principles*

| Stages and principles | | |
|---|---|---|
| **Stage 1**: <br> Problem formulation <br> • Perceive and define the problem scope <br> • Define the problem as a problem class | **Principle 1**: <br> Practice-inspired research | Applied research should prioritize real-world problems and focus on practical solutions |
| | **Principle 2**: <br> Theory-ingrained artifact | Solutions are informed by sound theories, guiding decision-making throughout the ADR iterations |
| **Stage 2**: <br> Building, intervention, and evaluation <br> • Continuous and interactive artifact design and evaluation <br> • Challenge existing ideas | **Principle 3**: Reciprocal shaping | Continually shaping artifacts enhances solution reliability that enables the systematic documentation of insights for knowledge creation and theory enhancement |
| | **Principle 4**: Mutually influential roles | The mutual learning effect between research participants supports the importance of stakeholder theory in the given context |
| | **Principle 5**: Authentic and concurrent evaluation | Continual evaluation of progress leads to intertwined analysis and design decisions throughout the process |

(continued)

**Table 2.1** (continued)

*Stages and principles*

| | | |
|---|---|---|
| **Stage 3:** Reflection and learning • Conceptually applied to the problem class | **Principle 6:** Guided emergence | The resultant artifacts embody the ongoing evolution from user perspectives that are influenced by authentic and concurrent evaluation, which include the prior principles, incorporated inputs, and experiences in a broader business problem context |
| **Stage 4:** Formalization of learning • Situated learning | **Principle 7:** Generalized outcomes | While acknowledging bespoke design, the significance of generalizing and abstracting research findings and generalized problems and solutions further highlights their applicability to broader contextual business problems |

*Source* Adapted from McCurdy et al. (2016) and Sein et al. (2011)

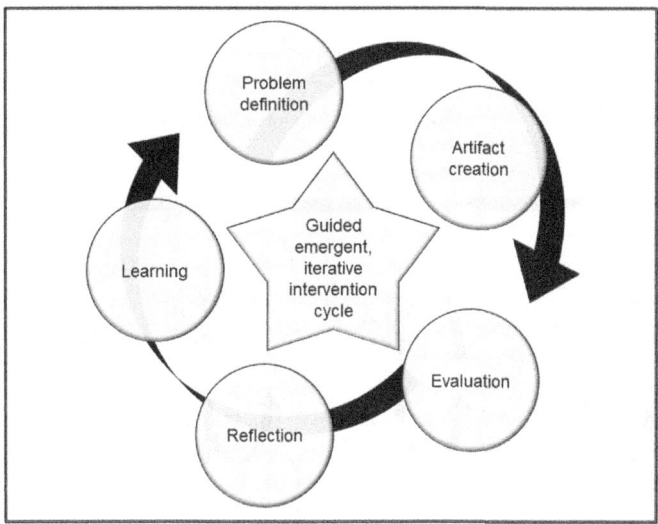

**Fig. 2.2** Iterative elaborated action design research cycle (*Source* Adapted from Mullarkey and Hevner 2018)

- A problem-centric diagnosis iteration that involves cycles to understand the domain area and its connection to the business problem in a comprehensive way.
- An object-centric design iteration that includes cycles to develop various design principles, features, models, and implementation approaches.
- A validation-centric implementation iteration consists of validation cycles to refine the actual construction and evaluation of the artifact.
- An observation-centric evolution iteration that concentrates on the continual refinement of the applied artifact to adapt to emerging realities and ensure optimal performance.

Mullarkey and Hevner (2018) note that the eADR process could be accessed at any stage, depending on the reality of the case. However, Sein and Rossi (2019) argue that the spirit of ADR emphasizes problem formulation, suggesting that the diagnosis phase should be the only entry point. Despite this argument, the eADR approach allows for revisiting

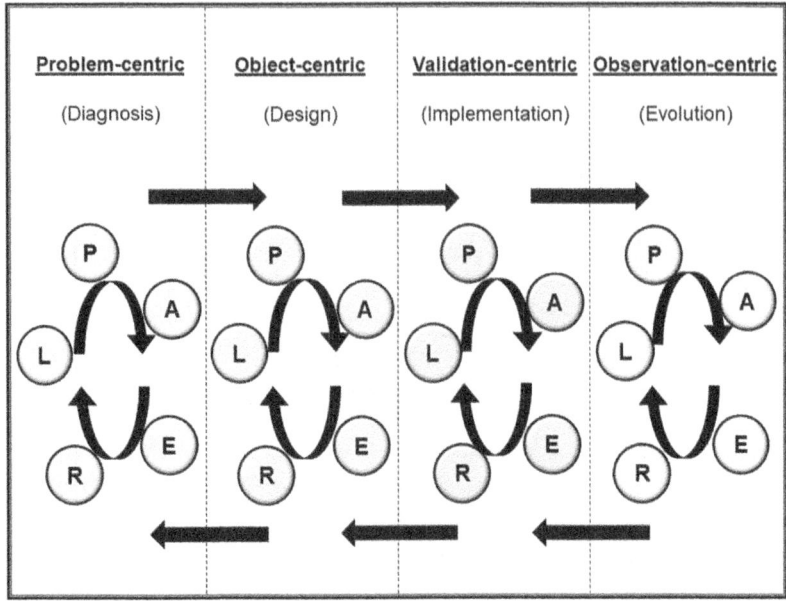

**Fig. 2.3** Elaborated action design research iterations (*Source* Adapted from Mullarkey and Hevner 2018)

earlier iterations if new facts and knowledge necessitates it, and multiple entry points are, therefore, conceptually enabled.

The crucial aspect of the highlighted approach lies in the development of an *artifact* to solve a business problem. The artifact concept refers to a human-made object that was created for use in a specific context. In business research, artifacts may encompass constructs, models, methods, and instantiations. Business management frameworks, models, and systems—including the managerial costing systems design model—could be considered artifacts in a design science research paradigm.

## 2.4   Research Team Composition

### 2.4.1   Introduction

Blumberg (2008) defines a target population as the encompassing group possessing specific characteristics that a research initiative tends to investigate. Conversely, a sample is a smaller selected group that represents the population and helps to understand its specific characteristics. While data saturation is essential for representation, there are no established guidelines for estimating sampling adequacy levels to achieve data saturation (Nieuwenhuis 2021). The ultimate sample size depends on the situation and should be sufficient for new information to emerge. Additionally, there is a difference between data saturation and theoretical saturation, where the latter encompasses identifying all main variations and phenomena in research findings (Nieuwenhuis 2021). In embarking on this iterative process with specific subject matter experts, aspects of a (mini-) Delphi research methodology were present. Nasa et al. (2021) state that the purpose of the Delphi technique is to generate a reliable consensus opinion from a group of experts by means of an iterative process in which the use of questions is interspersed with controlled feedback. In such a setting, there are typically multiple rounds of interaction with opportunities for feedback between the various iterations.

### 2.4.2   Industry Participants

In order to achieve the research objective of developing a model for effective managerial costing systems design, industry participants with knowledge of cost management and managerial costing systems, and experience in designing and implementing such systems were included. Industry practitioners meeting specific criteria were approached and invited to participate. The model was, therefore, developed and validated during iterative collaborations with two sets of industry practitioners (Table 2.2).

As indicated, the *Phase I team* included two senior executives from manufacturing/engineering organizations, plus the managing partner of an accounting and business consulting firm. These industry experts contributed their expertise and insights to the model's diagnosis and design iterations. The *Phase II team* included industry participants with expertise in designing and implementing managerial costing systems, and

**Table 2.2**   Research team composition

| Phase I Diagnosis and design iterations | A multinational European company that designs, manufactures, and distributes gear motors, drive systems, planetary gearboxes, and inverters for industrial automation, and mobile machinery. The researcher-practitioner team featured the managing director of the African division |
|---|---|
| | A United Kingdom-based global company renowned for manufacturing metal alloys and related products for diverse industrial and consumer applications. The researcher-practitioner team included the chief financial officer of the African division |
| | A South Africa-based accounting and business consulting firm with expertise in serving clients across various industries, including manufacturing, offering comprehensive professional consulting services. The researcher-practitioner team featured the managing partner of the firm |
| Phase II Implementation iteration | A privately owned engineering and manufacturing company located in South Africa's Vaal Triangle region, operating throughout the country. They have developed and deployed their own bespoke managerial costing system. The researcher-practitioner team included the company's owner and chief executive officer |
| | A Gauteng-based software consulting firm focused on enhancing business performances by designing value chain and managerial costing systems. They serve clients in Southern Africa and the Middle East. The researcher-practitioner team involved the firm's owner and senior managing consultant |

played a crucial role in validating the model during the implementation iteration.

Given the limited sample size, it is crucial to recognize that the opinions and experiences are specific to these industry practitioners. However, it is worth noting that the main emphasis was not on studying a particular industry, but on developing and validating a model able to guide the design of managerial costing systems. This was attained in collaboration with industry experts knowledgeable in the manufacturing industry and systems design. The concept of validity pertains to the ability of a solution design to accomplish its intended purpose. The research initiative adhered, therefore, to relevant design science criteria to ensure the desired validity and reliability of the process model and cost management framework. These criteria, as outlined by Hevner et al. (2004), included the following:

- An artifact is a construct, model, method, or instantiation unrelated to people or organizational elements.
- New knowledge is generated by addressing a specific business problem.
- The artifact should be valuable regarding functionality, performance, reliability, and usability.
- Research contributions should be evident through the artifact itself.
- Research should maintain rigor by following appropriate data collection and analysis techniques.
- Design is a process of exploration to find an effective problem solution.
- The solution needs to be communicated to relevant stakeholders.

### 2.4.3    Knowledge Development

Orlikowski and Iacono (2001) support the idea that (business) research methods should acknowledge that artifacts are influenced by the interests, values, and assumptions of various stakeholders involved in their development, investment, and use. The approach employed in this book differs from the typical use of a measuring instrument. Instead, the emphasis was on methodology and its focus on gathering specific information to facilitate data collection, analysis, and the development of new knowledge and, ultimately, the process model. Through researcher-practitioner interactions guided by a literature review, the objectives were clarified and analyzed. These interactions also provided an opportunity to delve deeper into the information to gather detailed insights.

The interactions with industry participants were conducted separately and consisted of multiple sessions held at various locations. The initial discussions introduced the research objectives and background information was provided. Shared literary background knowledge was limited to minimize researcher bias, and allowed the experts to express their perspectives and knowledge freely. Subsequent interactions involved focused discussions for data collection that led to the development of the initial iteration-specific artifact. This *in-process artifact* was then shared with the

experts for further input and refinement. Once the iteration-specific artifact reached a satisfactory level with all of the participants, the solution
development progressed to the next eADR iteration.

For the context of this book, the resultant model's validity was determined by the successful application of the eADR process that yielded the
following outcomes:

- The eADR approach resulted in the creation of a model that
  supports the development of effective managerial costing systems.
- Each chapter's eADR iteration refines the problem and involves
  reflection on the generated knowledge and the formalization thereof.
- The overall validity includes diagnostic and design validity that
  was established by input from industry experts familiar with operational cost management practices, while implementation validity
  was confirmed by industry experts experienced in managerial costing
  systems design and implementation.
- The systematic iteration of the eADR process ensured that the artifact's research contributions are valid, uphold scientific rigor, employ
  design as the research approach, and effectively communicate with
  relevant stakeholders.

## 2.5   In Conclusion

This chapter aimed to unpack and justify the chosen research design and
method by providing a roadmap that addressed the problem and objectives and achieved the design criteria. The design aspect highlighted the
philosophical and theoretical foundations, while the methods component
explained the tools used to answer the research problem. Within the
context of a design science paradigm, the ADR methodology and eADR
approach was justified as appropriate. The chapter concluded with reflections on validity and methodological rigor. The role and function of the
researcher-practitioner team in the execution of the research were of the
utmost importance in providing such rigor. The next chapter focuses on
enhancing problem comprehension, the initial diagnosis, and creating the
first iteration of the model design.

# References

Blumberg, B. 2008. *Business research methods*. 2nd ed. London: McGraw-Hill.

Cronholm, S. and Göbel, H. 2019. Evaluation of action design research. *Scandinavian Journal of Information Systems*, 31(2):35–82.

Ebersön, L., Eloff. I. and Ferreira, R. 2021. First steps in action research. In: Maree, K., ed. *First steps in research*: 2nd ed. Pretoria: Van Schaik Publishers. pp. 158–182.

Hevner, A.R., March, S.T. and Park, J. 2004. Design science in information systems research. *MIS Quarterly*, 28(1):75–105.

Iivari, J. and Venable, J.R. 2009. Action research and design science research— Seemingly similar but decisively dissimilar. Proceedings of the European Conference on Information Systems (ECIS) 2009. p. 73.

Järvinen, P. 2007. Action research is similar to design science. *Quality & Quantity*, 41:37–54.

Kessler, E.H., ed. 2013. *Encyclopedia of management theory*. Los Angeles: Sage.

Kivunja, C. and Kuyini, A.B. 2017. Understanding and applying research paradigms in educational contexts. *International Journal of Higher Education*, 6(5):26–41.

McCurdy, N., Dykes, J. and Meyer, M. 2016. Action design research and visualization design. Proceedings of the sixth workshop on Beyond Time and Errors on Novel Evaluation Methods for Visualization. October, Pages 10–18. https://doi.org/10.1145/2993901.2993916.

Mouton, J. 2011. *How to succeed in your master's and doctoral studies: A South African guide and resource book*. Pretoria: Van Schaik.

Mullarkey, M. and Hevner, A. 2018. An elaborated action design research process model. *European Journal of Information Systems*, 28(1):6–20.

Nasa, P., Jain. R. and Juneja, D. 2021. Delphi methodology in health care research: How to decide its appropriateness: *World Journal of Methodology*, 11(4):116–129. https://doi.org/10.5662/wjm.v11.i4.116.

Nieuwenhuis, J. 2021. Qualitative research designs and data-gathering techniques. In: Maree, K., ed. *First steps in research*: 2nd ed. Pretoria: Van Schaik Publishers. pp. 80–116.

Orlikowski, W.J. and Iacono, C.S. 2001. Research commentary: Desperately seeking the 'IT' in IT research—A call to theorizing the IT artefact. *Information Systems research*, 12(2):121–134.

Petersson, A.M. and Lundberg, J. 2016. Applying action design research (ADR) to develop concept generation and selection methods. *Procedia CIRP*, 50:222–227.

Pondy, L.R. and Mitroff, I.L. 1979. Beyond open system models of organization. *Research in Organizational Behaviour*, 1:3–39.

Sein, M.K., Henfridsson, O., Purao, S., Rossi, M. and Lindgren, R. 2011. Action design research. *MIS Quarterly*, 35(1):37–56.

Sein, M.K. and Rossi, M. 2019. Elaborating ADR while drifting away from its essence: A commentary on Mullarkey and Hevner. *European Journal of Information Systems*, 28(1):21–25.

Ward, E., Middelberg, S.L. and Buys. P.W. 2023. Developing a channeling framework for healthcare service provider networks for a medical scheme in South Africa. In: Buys, P. and Oberholzer, M., eds. *Business research: An illustrative guide to practical methodological applications in selected studies*. Palgrave Macmillan, pp. 313–334.

# CHAPTER 3

# Systems Thinking Foundation

The preceding chapter provided a contextualized overview of the methodology with the aim of achieving the objectives outlined in this book. This chapter shifts its focus toward the literature foundation of the model, specifically exploring the concept of *systems thinking* within its relevant context. By initially delving into systems theory, the groundwork is provided for probing deeper into the realms of systems engineering and cybernetics.

## 3.1 Background

In their seminal work, Mitroff et al. (1974) contend that the advent of the machine age facilitated the identification of interrelated, cohesive, but narrowly defined specialized fields including systems engineering, cybernetics, and operations research. These fields were all dedicated to comprehending an increasing number of realities within the context of organizational operations. Dekkers (2015) categorizes machinery, houses, companies, computers, organisms, and ecological networks as systems, while Yang et al. (2020) believe systems theory is fundamental to modern social science theory. Nortrup (2021) agrees with this perspective, stating that organizations operate as socio-technical systems within a larger socio-technical context. While supporting these claims, Kessler (2013) posits that systems theory transcends organizational and management theories

© The Author(s), under exclusive license to Springer Nature Singapore Pte Ltd. 2024
P. W. Buys, *Crafting Efficiency in Managerial Costing System Design*,
https://doi.org/10.1007/978-981-97-0934-2_3

by encompassing concepts ranging from microscopic cells to cosmic and metaphysical levels. The notion of a general systems theory could, therefore, be considered more of a *paradigm* rather than a distinct theory in its own right.

However, for the scope of this book, we embraced a perspective rooted in systems thinking that acknowledges the intricacies of management and the enduring repercussions of managerial decisions and choices on a multitude of interconnected stakeholders. Consequently, we contend that systems theory presents a holistic framework for comprehending organizational systems with a specific focus on managerial costing systems.

## 3.2   Systems Theory

Nortrup (2021) defines a system as a cohesive entity comprising interrelated elements with functional interdependencies—underscoring the significance of comprehending the intricate relationships among the system elements. Dekkers (2015) also highlights that comprehending a system may vary depending on the situation under consideration. We begin our exploration of systems by focusing on the concepts of system classification, its underlying principles, and the framework for systems design.

### 3.2.1   Systems Classification

De Wee (2021) and Van Schmidt et al. (2021) classify various system types, including physical, biological, designed, abstract, social, and human activity systems, to facilitate differentiation between them. Similarly, Blanchard and Fabrycky (2014) categorize systems classes within a contextual framework as follows:

- Natural systems arise from biological processes and exhibit inherent order and equilibrium, while artificial systems result from human intervention and design.
- Physical systems have a tangible form composed of physical components, whereas conceptual systems are represented symbolically on paper or digitally.
- Closed systems function in isolation from their external environments, whereas *open systems* actively engage with the external

environment that enable the exchange of material, energy, and information across system boundaries.

In the realm of business management, effectively managing organizational costs requires coordination among multiple departments, divisions, stakeholders and processes (Buys 2021). The managerial costing system should, therefore, encompass all these elements and relationships—serving as a crucial tool for evaluating organizational performance. Given this context, the model and subsequent managerial costing systems are viewed as artificial, conceptual open systems.

### 3.2.2   Systems Fundamentals

The primary objective of systems is to alter material, energy, or information by requiring specific inputs and engaging in processing activities, which subsequently yield an output (Blanchard and Fabrycky 2014) while occurring within clearly defined boundaries and encompassing various components and subsystems (Potts et al. 2020). As illustrated below, a system operates within a defined environment by consistently receiving inputs and generating outputs. It is crucial to emphasize that every systems component must maintain a relationship with at least one other component within the system (Fig. 3.1).

Systems-related design objectives include a range of goals, such as optimizing current system parameters and features, modifying system structures, or developing a completely new system. Rouissat et al. (2021) present two distinct approaches to understanding systems: A *structural* view that highlights components and subsystems; and a *dynamic* view that centers around a sequence of processes, such as activities and functions. These approaches could be further complemented by considering two additional dimensions. Firstly, a holistic perspective that emphasizes the overall system as a whole. Secondly, the focus could be directed toward individual system attributes, which could involve studying the components within the system or analyzing the relationships within the system.

In a given context, a system could be categorized based on its state and purpose, which pertain to the characteristics and relationships of the system itself or its constituents (Blanchard and Fabrycky 2014). System classification often relies, therefore, on the behavioral characteristics exhibited by the system. It helps to differentiate between *static*

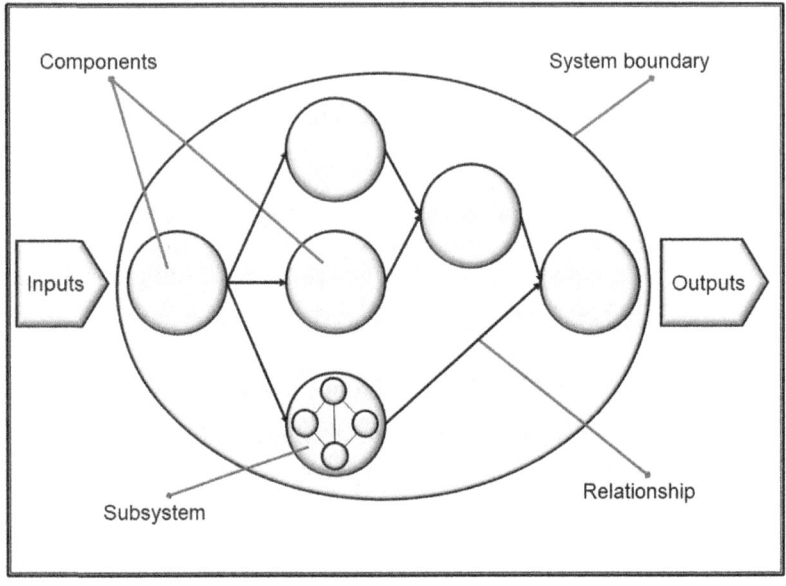

**Fig. 3.1**  Conceptual systems environment

*systems*, which lack operating components in their structural design, and remain unaltered over a defined period, and *dynamic systems*, which incorporate both structural components and operating components that allow them to adapt and modify in response to specific triggers (Alizadeh and Soulgani 2021). It is crucial to acknowledge that no system, regardless of whether it is a static system with limited interaction with its environment, could be entirely isolated from its external surroundings. Over time, a static system undergoes changes, as inputs (material, energy, or information) enter its boundary and corresponding outputs exit it. Consequently, although the model within the context of this book's overall structure may remain static based on its design parameters, substantial interaction with organizational subsystems and stakeholders may occur. This interaction would impact the quality of inputs and the desired output requirements. The envisaged process model and any subsequent managerial costing systems developed from this point onward, could thus be characterized as dynamic.

### 3.2.3 System Design Framework

In any research undertaking, establishing and fully understanding the intended research goals and objectives is of the utmost importance. This principle applies equally to systems research and design. Without a clear vision for the desired system, the design process may result in ineffective and obsolete systems and components.

- System hierarchy: In an organizational context, Pondy and Mitroff (1979) adopt Kenneth Boulding's *hierarchy of systems complexity*, comprising nine levels: frameworks, clockworks, control systems, open systems, blueprinted control systems, internal image systems, symbol processing systems, multi-cephalous systems, and systems of unspecified complexity. Managerial costing system design is particularly relevant at the last two levels, where organizational systems consist of groups of individuals, potentially introducing new complexities that have not yet been fully understood. From a slightly different perspective, Blanchard and Fabrycky (2014) propose a comprehensive hierarchical framework that elucidates the relationships between systems—encompassing both natural and artificial domains. At the lowest level, *static structures* exist, ranging from atomic scales to the vast expanse of the universe. Progressing upward, we encounter *simple dynamic systems*, which incorporate elements of movement and *cybernetic systems*, which involve the transmission and interpretation of information. Moving further, we observe *cell and open systems*, displaying signs of life, followed by plants and genetic-societal systems that showcase differentiated and interdependent components. Finally, *animal systems* emerge that feature mobility, purposeful behavior, and self-awareness. Within *human systems*, there exists a progression of sophistication, ranging from basic self-awareness to intricate *social-organizational* systems encompassing roles, communication channels, value systems, and other characteristics unique to humans. Additionally, there are *transcendental systems* that delve into philosophical and spiritual aspects rather than focusing solely on empirical and material elements. It is important to note that this perspective on system levels should be viewed within a multidimensional context, where higher-level systems build upon concepts from lower-level systems. When it comes to managerial costing systems, certain aspects, such as management structures, may remain relatively stable, but occasionally display dynamism. However, the crux of effective cost management lies in the transmission and interpretation of information. The understanding of the cybernetic systems level is likely, therefore, crucial in comprehending the hierarchical classification of anticipated outcomes in this book.

- System building blocks: In system design, it is crucial to grasp the constituent elements and their relationships as fundamental building blocks. Blanchard and Fabrycky (2014) emphasize the components and relationship aspects in the context of systems. Firstly, *system components* could be classified into three categories: (i) structural components that define the system's layout and arrangement; (ii) operating components that handle the processing within the system; and (iii) flow components that involve the modification of materials, energy, or information by the system's processes. Secondly, the *relationships* among interconnected components should be designed to support the system's objectives. These relationships could be categorized as (i) symbiotic relationships, which are functionally vital for the proper functioning of linked components; (ii) synergistic relationships, which complement symbiotic relationships and enhance the system's performance; and (iii) redundant relationships, which involve duplicate components and serve as backups in case of system failure. Understanding systems requires recognizing the importance of functional relationships among elements, and a system could not be considered as such if it consists only of unrelated elements. For the purpose of this book, the model assists in the identification and classification of components, attributes, and relationships within managerial costing systems.

- System analysis approach: The aforementioned concepts propose that system components have the potential to be systems on their own, and that a system could also function as a constituent of a larger system. Furthermore, a system operating at one hierarchical level has the capability to serve as a subsystem or component at a different level. Consequently, the concepts of systems and subsystems are interconnected. Bearing this in consideration, we could identify distinct methodologies in the analysis and design of systems, such as:

- A *black box* approach that focuses on the external relationships between a system and its environment with the aim
  of understanding the system's overall behavior in response to
  changes.
- An *aggregate strata* approach that emphasizes the analysis of
  internal structures and relationships within a system, distinguishing between systems, subsystems, components, and their
  interconnections or relationships. This approach facilitates the
  categorization of observations into various levels of aggregation
  that enable the examination of interactions and relationships
  among subsystems or components.

Figure 3.2 illustrates the analysis levels pertaining to our emphasis on the
design of an effective managerial costing system.

According to the aforementioned conceptual illustration, the black box
level examines the connections between the financial system and other

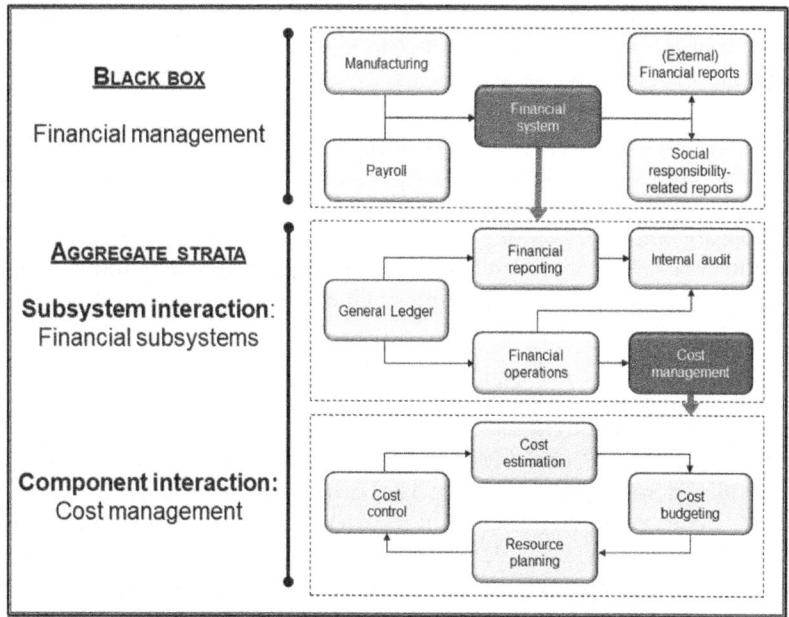

**Fig. 3.2**  Analysis level: managerial costing system design

organizational systems. The financial system receives inputs from functions like payroll and manufacturing, and it, in turn, provides inputs to corporate reporting and corporate social responsibility functions. Progressing to the next level, the first aggregate strata level explores the functional interactions between financial subsystems and the cost management subsystem, including the general ledger and financial operations. At the second aggregate strata level, the focus shifts to the relationships and interactions among different components of cost management, such as cost estimation, budgeting, planning and control. All three approaches must be incorporated into the overall design approach to address management scenarios effectively, due to the integrated nature and complexity of cost management.

## 3.3   SYSTEMS ENGINEERING

As one of the original thought leaders of *scientific management*, Taylor (1934) argued that it is not a science per se, but rather the application of systematic methods in an organizational and systems management context. Confirming such, Bertrand and Fransoo (2002) consider scientific management as a characteristic found within the engineering profession. Management systems that are engineered appropriately derive enhanced value from the interconnections among their constituent parts, surpassing the mere aggregation of individual components. When dealing with managerial costing systems, which are characterized by their complexity and integration, adopting an engineering mindset proves advantageous. This approach involves contemplating the definition, application, and methodology of systems engineering.

### 3.3.1   *Defining Systems Engineering*

To shed light on the intricate task of defining systems engineering, this book addresses the challenges arising from the inherent vagueness in determining system effectiveness. This concept could be traced back to Henry Bode, a prominent figure in the early days of systems engineering, who described it as a nebulous subject. The National Research Council (1967) supports the notion that systems engineering is better understood within a broad and adaptable framework. Hence, the following illustrative perspectives are presented to explore the definition of systems engineering:

- The Institute of Industrial and Systems Engineers (IISE, n.d.) defines it as "*concerned with the design, improvement, and installation of integrated systems of people, materials, information, equipment, and energy.*"
- The International Council on Systems Engineering (INCOSE, n.d.) defines systems engineering as "*a transdisciplinary and integrative approach to enable the successful realization, use, and retirement of engineered systems, using systems principles and concepts, and scientific, technological, and management methods.*"
- Kirkpatrick (2021) views it as a systematic, interdisciplinary methodology encompassing system design, realization, technical management, operations, and retirement.
- Bobrek et al. (2020) describe systems engineering as an interdisciplinary approach and method that aims to ensure the successful engineering of complex systems.

In the realm of engineering, systems engineering is, therefore, regarded as an extensive and adaptable concept that embraces a holistic methodology for designing systems that encompass diverse technical and social domains.

### 3.3.2    Application of Systems Engineering

Based on the information provided, it appears that there is a consensus on the wide applicability of systems engineering concepts across different contexts and environments. In our case, systems engineering is viewed as the practical implementation of systemic disciplines to address the complexities present in modern technology, organizations, and society. Blanchard and Fabrycky (2014) emphasize the importance of considering systems engineering from two perspectives: Application areas and application domain. The *application areas* encompass diverse sectors, such as communications, healthcare, education, power generation, and aerospace, with a primary focus on the manufacturing sector in this book. The *application domain* pertains to the specific characteristics of the system itself, including its scale (large or small), its affiliation (private or governmental), and whether it aims to enhance existing systems. This book predominantly concentrates on newly designed, complex systems that highlight the domain aspect.

In diverse scenarios, the fundamental principles of design and development continue to apply, regardless of the varying extent and complexity of engineering efforts. Recent research in systems engineering encompasses various areas. Elliot et al. (2013) focused on overcoming barriers to applying engineering systems in the rail sector. Bobrek et al. (2020) explored the applicability of systems engineering in the design of university study programs. Teslia et al. (2020) developed engineering concepts for digitalizing higher education institutions. Zubowski (2020) examined the management challenges involved in configuring model-based system engineering for multiple variant aircraft fleets.

To summarize, systems engineering concepts transcend conventional engineering fields and hold value in social sciences, particularly in management. The application of a systems engineering-based methodology is expected to enhance the design quality of managerial costing systems.

### 3.3.3    Systems Engineering Methodology

According to Kirkpatrick (2021) and Philbin (2021), systems engineering involves the design, integration, and management of complex systems throughout their life cycles. Rodriguez-Martinez et al. (2018) propose that a systems engineering methodology includes a requirement analysis, design, construction, and operations. We can, therefore, characterize systems engineering as a sequential process encompassing various phases typically entailing a (full) *life cycle* perspective that includes the design, feasibility, development, production, use, and withdrawal aspects. Consequently, the comprehensive planning of the entire development process assumes utmost importance. A well-thought-out *requirements definition* emphasizing specific design criteria would, therefore, ensure a proper understanding of the system's objective and purpose, thereby necessitating an *integrated design* approach that considers all relevant stakeholders and affected areas. It is essential to integrate the system components and enable successful functioning. To optimize the addressing of design objectives, an *interdisciplinary approach* involving collaboration among experts from different domains must be incorporated. Finally, larger projects may require analysis and design throughout their life cycle, making it crucial to identify and consider all critical phases from system design and development to operations, maintenance, and disposal.

Systems engineering prioritizes, therefore, the systematic application of a methodology that facilitates scientific modeling, testing, problem identification, rectification, implementation, and evaluation. Confirming the views of Bertrand and Fransoo (2002), Yearworth (2019) noted that systems engineering principles are now an essential part of management sciences. As such, systems engineering is considered the facilitator of a design process that incorporates relevant principles for the development of an effective managerial costing system design. Hence, the systematic approach embedded in eADR, the iterations of which enable a (i) well-thought-out requirements definition, (ii) integrated and interdisciplinary process that is (iii) cognizant of the overall system life cycle, is an embodiment of systems engineering in the context of this book.

## 3.4   Cybernetics

During the emotionally challenging World War II era, several intellectual disciplines emerged, among them artificial intelligence and cybernetics. Although closely related, these disciplines have distinct goals: Artificial intelligence seeks to create computers with human-like intelligence, while cybernetics focuses on developing goal-oriented systems capable of adapting to dynamic environments. Given that this book aims to develop a *managerial costing system* with specific objectives, it takes into account the concepts, principles, and management aspects associated with the cybernetics concept.

### 3.4.1   Cybernetic Concept

Norbert Wiener's endeavors during World War II to construct an *anti-aircraft predictor machine*, capable of forecasting aircraft trajectories, could be identified as the inception of modern cybernetics (Galison 1994). Despite its lack of success, Wiener's objective was to design a machine with the ability to anticipate human actions. Simultaneously, conferences sponsored by the Josiah Macy Jr. Foundation played a significant role in advancing cybernetics as a scientific field, covering a range of social and cognitive scientific disciplines (Pickering 2013).

Yang et al. (2020) assert that cybernetics, along with systems theory and information theory, constitutes a cornerstone in the field of social sciences. Pickering (2013) discusses Stafford Beer (1959), who distinguished between the physical sciences, which focus on *knowable systems*, and cybernetics, which is regarded as a science of *complex systems*. Nortrup (2021) elaborates and argues that the origins of systems thinking could be found in sociology and cybernetics. Hence, the fundamental idea of cybernetics embodies a multidisciplinary and purposeful scientific approach that aims to replicate human cognitive abilities in order to achieve specific objectives. This highlights a vital aspect of this book namely, *recognizing* that managerial costing systems play a pivotal role in an organization's pursuit of value creation and economic viability goals, making effective cost management, therefore, achievable.

### 3.4.2    Cybernetic Principles

Engaging relevant stakeholders, considering various options, re-framing problems, and searching for common ground could be facilitated by embracing systems thinking. This is particularly important in the integrated nature of designing managerial costing systems, where multiple role-players from diverse departments operate with their own objectives and requirements. Within this particular framework, Blanchard and Fabrycky (2014) view cybernetics as a comprehensive field that incorporates the principles of self-regulation (servo theory), which include control, output, and feedback. Yang et al. (2020) concur with this perspective, affirming the organized and controlled nature of cybernetic systems when describing the cybernetic systems view. Taking into account these viewpoints, we conclude that the fundamental principle of cybernetics relies on its ability to adapt to unfamiliar circumstances. Put simply, it exemplifies (i) the necessity for specific inputs to generate desired outputs in order to accomplish a specific objective; and (ii) the ongoing monitoring and adjustment of the system's processes, including environmental information to ensure the attainment of the desired output goals. Presented in Fig. 3.3 is a conceptual depiction showcasing the self-regulatory and adaptive capacities required when striving toward a goal.

As illustrated, in contemporary cybernetic theory, *feedback* is a crucial concept that allows for the identification and implementation of corrective actions when specific system components fail to contribute to the desired goals (Havlova 2015). Within more complex systems, the integration of the feedback concept gives rise to the potential existence of multiple cybernetic loops within both subsystems and the overall system (as illustrated in Fig. 3.4).

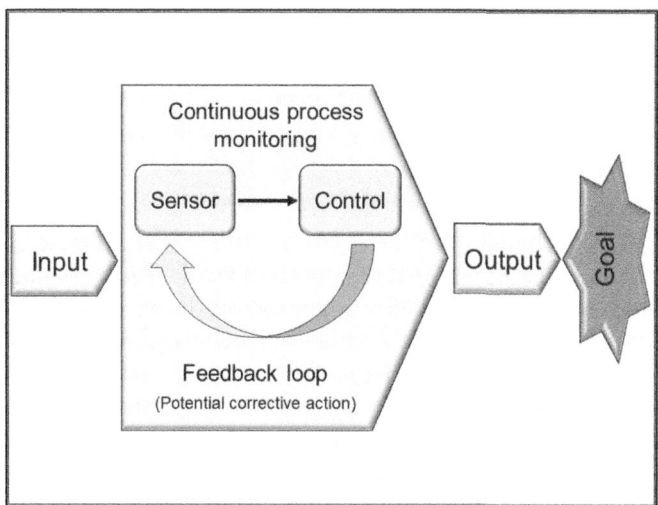

**Fig. 3.3** Conceptual cybernetic feedback loop

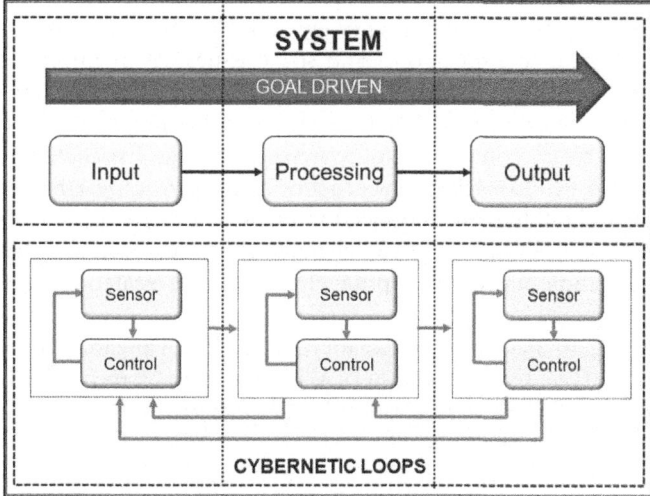

**Fig. 3.4** Systems-wide cybernetic feedback loops

Given the aforementioned points, our comprehension of cybernetic ontology involves acknowledging the interconnectedness between systems and stakeholders, and recognizing the challenges associated with managing complex systems.

### 3.4.3    Management Cybernetics

Although officially emerging in the 1940s, the roots of cybernetics could be traced back to the ancient philosopher Plato, who introduced the term κυβερνητική (kybernētikḗ), meaning governance or steering. This connection to management is emphasized by Blanchard and Fabrycky (2014) as well as Pangaro (2013). Furthermore, Yang et al. (2020) suggest that cybernetics offers a set of tools that could be utilized in economic development strategies, thereby making it relevant to the field of management sciences. Additionally, its cognitive scientific approach, which places emphasis on deriving insights from past experiences, holds significance in the realm of management sciences.

The concept of cybernetics in relation to management involves recognizing that systems thinking emerged from the belief that adopting a comprehensive approach to psychology and biology could aid in understanding complex organizational and social issues. As mentioned earlier, cybernetics could be viewed as the discipline concerned with purposeful and optimal control within complex systems, including organizations, and it forms a crucial component of systems thinking. Expanding on this idea, Jackson (2003) defines cybernetics as the *science of effective organizations*, and established a connection between cybernetics and the field of management. Dekkers (2015) characterizes management cybernetics as the application of cybernetic principles to human-created organizations and their interactions.

According to Blanchard and Fabrycky (2014), Pangaro (2013), and Pickering (2013), the publication of Wiener's book "*Cybernetics: Control and Communication in the Animal and Machine*" in 1948 marked a significant turning point, leading to the widespread acceptance of the term 'cybernetics'. According to Buys (2021), the subtitle of Wiener's book encapsulates two vital principles central to the field of cybernetics:

- Firstly, the cybernetic concept has made significant contributions to systems thinking, primarily by emphasizing the importance of information, control, and communication. It recognizes the crucial role of information flow and underscores the importance of feedback control principles. These concepts are in alignment with the objective of cost and management accounting, which entails measuring, analyzing, and reporting pertinent information to facilitate decision-making.

- Secondly, cybernetics recognizes that both biological and technological systems function according to their respective principles. Practitioners employ feedback models, goals, and information flow to understand the capabilities of these systems. Concerning cost management, managerial information is generated within a technological environment and utilized within a biological (human) setting—highlighting the interaction between humans and machines. This interaction is particularly relevant in the era of the *Fourth Industrial Revolution*.

The management function is closely intertwined with the principles of cybernetics, specifically information communication, performance control, and a goal-driven approach. Consequently, the practice of cost management by accountants, engineers, and managers could be regarded as in harmony with the principles of cybernetics.

### 3.4.4   Managerial Theories

Progressing from this point, we delve into the realm of management theories. A perspective rooted in management cybernetics underscores the interdependence and mutual reinforcement of different management systems in the pursuit of organizational goals. Systems engineering plays a crucial role in understanding stakeholder requirements and devising solutions to address problems. Emphasizing the importance of establishing a requirements baseline with stakeholders, this book introduces two pertinent management theories that augment the notion of cybernetics within the domain of managerial costing systems.

- Stakeholder theory emphasizes the significance of all stakeholders, beyond solely shareholders, in order to achieve effective organizational functioning and value generation. It places emphasis on the organizational elements that contribute to effectiveness, especially when considering the organization as a system. The theory validates managers' decision-making roles and provides a framework for justi-fying business activities and operations. Within this theory, there are multiple essential considerations that merit attention, which include:

- Legitimate stakeholders with vested interests in the organi-zation's operations and consequences, play a pivotal role in enabling the achievement of its objectives (Camilleri 2018).
- Ethical and governance practices are in accordance with the principles of leadership ethics, placing a strong emphasis on them (Subramanian 2018).
- Value creation that originates from the sustainable utilization of an organization's asset base. While agency theory primarily focuses on the maximization of shareholder value, stakeholder theory broadens the notion of value by incorporating the utility delivered to a wider array of stakeholders (Kessler 2013).

- Stewardship theory presents a behavior model based on an organi-zation's intrinsic values, as proposed by Camilleri (2018). Menyah (2013) suggests that all employees should strive toward enhancing the well-being of organizational stakeholders. However, Adams et al. (2016) hold a differing opinion, asserting that stewards are typically managers who prioritize sustainable organizational value. In this book, we recognize elements from both perspectives, viewing stewardship theory as complementary to stakeholder theory. Our argument emphasizes that organizational sustainability encom-passes more than just economic value creation, and asserts that all employees bear stewardship responsibility. Rather than relying on control and rules, we propose collaboration as the means to attain organizational objectives, encouraging cooperative behaviors that benefit multiple stakeholders (Tillema and Ter Boght 2016). Conse-quently, a strong connection emerges between stewardship theory and corporate governance practices, suggesting that stewardship behavior leads to morally guided decision-making and exemplary governance practices.

To summarize, stakeholder theory—when seen from a systems perspec-tive—aims to incorporate diverse interests, while stewardship theory plays a supportive role. This perspective aligns with the cybernetic viewpoint, which emphasizes the significance of feedback, control, and goal-orientated principles to achieve optimal outcomes. Within this book, effective managerial costing systems extend beyond mere consideration of stakeholders. The cybernetic principles imply that stakeholder feedback should be analyzed and utilized to modify organizational strategies and operations as needed. Given that cost management is a vital function in management, it impacts and is influenced by various internal and external stakeholders. The aforementioned cybernetic principles are, therefore, inherent and essential in cost management to ensure effective organizational leadership.

## 3.5   In Conclusion

In this chapter, an exploration was undertaken on the perspectives of systems thinking as a fundamental approach to achieve effective cost management. The concepts of systems theory, systems engineering, and cybernetics were discussed. Systems theory emphasizes the relationships among the components of a system, serving as a guiding approach for a cost management analysis. Systems engineering was elucidated by presenting its core concepts, design framework, and scope to approach such systems' design. The discussion on cybernetics shed light on the vital role played by information communication, interpretation, and responsive actions. The significance of incorporating stakeholder feedback in the pursuit of management objectives was also highlighted. In the upcoming chapter, the complexities of business processes and related aspects in the context of effective cost management are thoroughly examined.

## References

Adams, C.A., Potter, B.S., Singh, P.J. and York, J. 2016. Exploring the implication of integrated reporting for social investment. *British Accounting Review*, 48(3):283–296.

Alizadeh, S. and Soulgani, B.S. 2021. Experimental investigation of the brine effect on asphaltene precipitation and deposition during water injection in porous media using static and dynamic systems. *Energy & Fuels*, 35(14):11141–11153. https://doi.org/10.1021/acs.energyfuels.1c00090.

Bertrand, J.W.M. and Fransoo, J.C. 2002. Operations management research methodologies using quantitative modeling. *International journal of operations and production management*, 22(2):241–264. https://doi.org/10.1108/01443570210414338.

Blanchard, B.S. and Fabrycky, W.J. 2014. *Systems engineering and analysis*. Essex: Pearson Education Limited.

Bobrek, M., Tanasić, Z. and Janjić, G. 2020. Systems engineering methodologies for study program development. Annals of the Faculty of Engineering Hunedora—*International Journal of Engineering*, 18(4):29–32.

Buys, P.W. 2021. Introduction. In: Buys, P.W., ed. *Designing cost management systems to support business decision-making*. Singapore: Palgrave MacMillan. pp. 1–10.

Camilleri, MA. 2018. Theoretical insight on integrated reporting: The inclusion of nonfinancial capitals in corporate disclosures. *Corporate Communication: An International Journal*, 10(2):1–22. https://doi.org/10.1108/CCIJ-01-2018-0016.

Dekkers, R. 2015. *Applied systems theory*. Heidelberg: Springer International Publishing.

De Wee, G. 2021. Comparative policy analysis and the science of conceptual systems: A candidate pathway to a common variable. *Foundations of Science*. https://doi.org/10.1007/s10699-021-09782-5.

Elliot, B., O'Neil, A., Roberts, C., Schmid, F. and Shannon, I. 2013. Overcoming barriers to transferring systems engineering practices into the rail sector. *Systems Engineering*, 15(2):203–212.

Galison, P. 1994. The ontology of the enemy: Norbet Wiener and the cybernetic vision. *Critical Enquiry*, 21:228–266.

Havlova, K. 2015. What integrated reporting changed: The case study of early adopters. *Procedia Economics and Finance*, 34(1):231–237.

IISE (Institute of industrial and systems engineers). n.d. *What is industrial and systems engineering?* https://www.iise.org/Details.aspx?id=282. Date of access: 18 Sept. 2020.

INCOSE (International Council on Systems Engineering). n.d. Systems Engineering. https://www.incose.org/about-systems-engineering/system-and-se-definition/systems-engineering-definition. Date of access: 18 Sept. 2020.

Jackson, M.C. 2003. *Systems thinking: Creative Holism for managers*. Wiley: University of Hull, UK.

Kessler, E.H., ed. 2013. *Encyclopaedia of management theory*. Sage reference, Pace University.

Kirkpatrick, R. 2021. Systems engineering and chemical engineering design. *The Chemical Engineer*, December 2020/January 2021:34–37.

Menyah, T. 2013. Stewardship theory and shareholder. *Australian Journal of Management*, 9(1):5–22.

Mitroff, I.L., Betz, F., Pondy, L.A. and Sagasti, F. 1974. On managing science in the systems age: Two schemas for the study of science as a whole systems phenomenon. *Interfaces*, 4(3):46–58.

National Research Council. 1967. *Applied science and technological progress: A report to the committee on science and astronautics, US House of Representatives*. Washington, DC: The National Academies Press. https://doi.org/10.17226/21281.

Nortrup, K. 2021. Systems thinking is vital in today's world. *ISE Magazine*, 53(2):26.

Pangaro, P. 2013. 'Getting started' guide to Cybernetics. https://www.pangaro.com/definition-cybernetics.html. Date of access: 31 March 2020.

Philbin, S.P. 2021. Driving sustainability through engineering management and systems engineering. *Sustainability*, 13:1–7. https://doi.org/10.3390/su1 3126687.

Pickering, A. 2013. Cybernetics. In: Friis, J.K.B.O., Pederson, S.A. and Hendricks, V.F., eds. *A companion to the philosophy of technology*. West Sussex: Wiley-Blackwell. pp. 118–122.

Pondy, L.R. and Mitroff, I.L. 1979. Beyond open system models of organization. *Research in organizational behaviour*, 1:3–39.

Potts, M.W., Sartor, P.A., Johnson, A. and Bullock, S. 2020. Assaying the importance of system complexity for the systems engineering community. *Systems Engineering*, 23:579–596.

Rodriguez-Martinez, L.C., Duran-Limon, H.A., Mora, M. and Rodriguez, F.A. 2018. SOCA-DESM: A well-structured SOCA development systems engineering methodology. *Computer Science and Information Systems*, 16(1):19–44. 10.CSIS170703035R

Rouissat, B., Bekkouche, A. and Smail, N. 2021. Contribution of the requirements engineering to the evaluation of water resources systems efficiency. *Applied Water Science*, 11:29. https://doi.org/10.1007/s13201-021-013 59-8.

Subramanian, S. 2018. Stewardship theory of corporate governance and value system. *Indian Journal of Corporate Governance*, 11(1):88–102.

Taylor, F.W. 1934. *The principles of scientific management*. New York and London: Harper & Bros.

Teslia, I., Yehorchenkova, N., Khlevna, I., Kataieva, Y., Latysheva, T., Yehorchenkov, O., Khlevnyi, A. and Veretelnyk, V. 2020. Developing a systems engineering concept for digitalizing higher education institutions. *Eastern-European Journal of Enterprise Technologies*, 6(2 (108)):6–20. https://doi.org/10.15587/1729-4061.2020.219260.

Tillema, S. and Ter Boght, H.J. 2016. Does an agency-type of audit model fit a stewardship context? Evidence from performance auditing in Dutch municipalities. *Financial Accountability and Management*, 32(2):135–156.

Van Schmidt, N.D., Oviedo, J.L., Hruska, T., Huntsinger, L., Kovach, T.J., Kilpatrick, A., Miller, N.L. and Beissinger, S.R. 2021. Assessing impacts of social-ecological diversity on resilience in a wetland coupled human and natural system. *Ecology and Society*, 26(2):3. https://doi.org/10.5751/ES-12223-260203.

Yang, Y-J., Chen, C-C. and Chen, Y-T. 2020. New method of solving the economic complex systems. *Discrete Dynamics in Nature and Society*, vol. 2020, Article ID 8827544, 26 pages https://doi.org/10.1155/2020/882 7544.

Yearworth, M. 2019. The theoretical foundation(s) for systems engineering? *Systems Research and Behavioural Science*, 37:184–187.

Zubowski, D.R. 2020. Configuration management challenges of model based system engineering on multiple variant aircraft fleets. *Journal of Aviation/ Aerospace Education & Research*, 29(3):68–81.

# CHAPTER 4

# Business Process Considerations

The previous chapter emphasized the importance of the systems thinking concept in managerial costing systems. The current chapter will address the business process concept as the second pillar in the literature foundation. It will contextualize business processes and delve into business management and process modeling.

## 4.1 Background

Bhaskar (2018) asserts that organizations inherently have multiple business processes to create their products and services. Tarhan et al. (2016) further argue that an organizational focus is crucial for effective business process management, a viewpoint supported by Weske (2010), who sees a proper understanding of organizational operations as a fundamental goal in business process management. In context, Bronzo et al. (2013) discovered that analyzing business processes alone positively affects organizational performance. Ahmad and Soberi (2018) agree herewith when opining that mapping the value stream reveals potential wasteful activities. Even though a thorough understanding of the integrated business processes is vital, we also argue that the alignment thereof with organizational strategies is essential for business processes to create value.

Organizations dedicated to effective process management enhance their ability to integrate data flow, leading to process intelligence and

© The Author(s), under exclusive license to Springer Nature Singapore Pte Ltd. 2024
P. W. Buys, *Crafting Efficiency in Managerial Costing System Design*,
https://doi.org/10.1007/978-981-97-0934-2_4

understanding of the financial and cost implications, in turn resulting in financial intelligence. Effective and efficient business processes should also contribute to effective cost management. Cost management activities aid practical process management objectives and offer a performance measurement perspective on core processes. Business processes must be systematically analyzed and evaluated to achieve an integrated understanding. This underscores the significance of business process modeling, particularly concerning business processes, process management, and even process improvement initiatives, as unpacked in the sections below.

## 4.2   Definition of Business Process

In this section, foundational contexts in process modeling will be elucidated, including process levels, classification, life cycle, and improvements, to introduce the business operations perspective according to the book's second pillar.

### 4.2.1   Business Process Modeling

The concept of a business process can be defined as an activity triggered by an initiating event involving various role-players' events (Aldin and De Cesare 2011). It is a coordinated set of activities in an organizational and technical environment aimed at achieving a business objective through efficient resource consumption (Krogstie 2016). Operations and activities can be classified as manual, user interactions, or system activities (Aldin and De Cesare 2011), and processes are performed on different dynamic levels, requiring flexibility, knowledge creation, and knowledge emergence.

Modeling such processes would typically involve considering multiple aspects, including coordinated tasks and stakeholders. Herein the process model facilitates management to enhance or realign tasks and goals. Business process models can be categorized as descriptive, prescriptive, or explanatory and often serve as communication tools in support of flexibility and continuous improvement. Figure 4.1 shows a simplified business process modeling concept overview.

The figure demonstrates that the integration and coordination of tasks, pursuit of goals, effective management of resources, and consideration of legitimate stakeholders provide essential business process inputs for managing business processes. These business processes ultimately guide

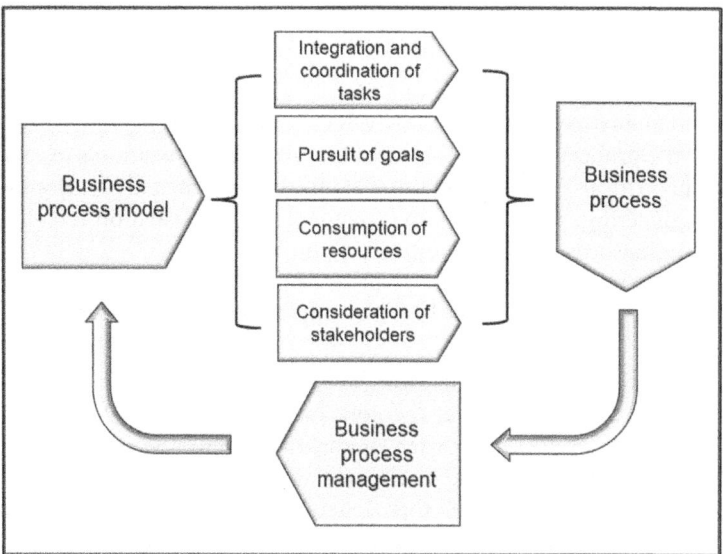

**Fig. 4.1**  Conceptual business process modeling

the management of tasks, resources, and stakeholders. A process model to guide managerial costing systems arguably includes all of the concepts and objectives mentioned in this section, speaking to integrated systems thinking, goal-driven cybernetics, and legitimate stakeholders.

### 4.2.2    Business Process Levels

Understanding business processes is crucial for designing cost management systems. Proper insight into the organization itself is fundamental in this regard. According to Duckert (2011), organizations often need to pay more attention to their primary function. In this regard, Bhaskar (2018) suggests that most organizational processes can be categorized into core processes related to product and service development, order generation and fulfillment, and customer services. Al-Shourah and Al-Shourah (2020) add to this that core business functions focus on customer satisfaction and are vital for the organization's continued existence and ability to create economic value.

The basic business structure consists of:

- The core business functions critical for the organization's existence and ability to create economic value, i.e., the being directly reflective of the primary (or initial) justification of the organization's existence.
- The critical support functions such as research and development, engineering, supply chain management, and information technology (IT), ensuring efficient core operations.
- The peripheral functions, such as legal, finance, accounting, and human resources, depend on a strong operational core.

Figure 4.2 illustrates this structure.

As illustrated in the figure, the core business processes should be the organization's key focus in order to ensure continuous, effective operations and are directly relevant to the managerial costing system according to the research objective. In this structure, conventional thinking may label cost management as a peripheral function under finance and accounting. Consequently, designing managerial costing systems is often an afterthought within many organizations. However, we argue that

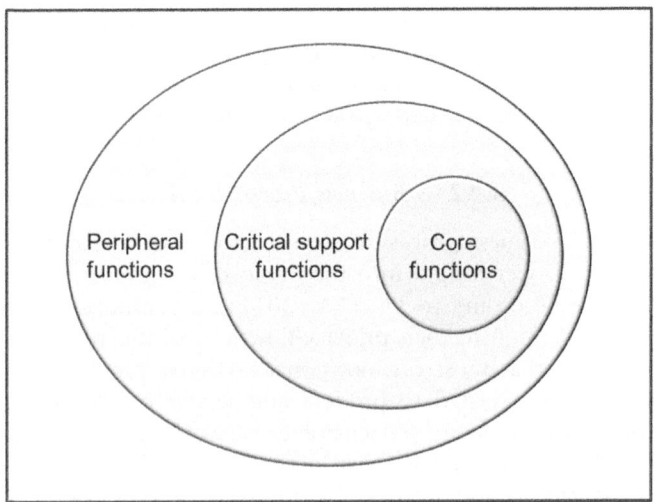

**Fig. 4.2**  Conceptual business process levels

effective cost management goes beyond cost accounting, significantly impacting cash generation and resource utilization. Thus, cost management is more than a peripheral function and should be classified as a critical support function. In fact, it could be considered part of research and development, engineering, and supply chain functions, given its importance and the need for a thorough analysis and understanding of business processes. This may be attained by the classification of the business processes as applicable in the organizational context.

### 4.2.3 Business Process Classification

An organization comprises interconnected product delivery processes (Duckert 2011), which reflect its behavior (Aldin and De Cesare 2011). Business processes could arguably be classified based on dimensions such as managerial processes for governance, operational processes for production and delivery, and supporting processes for finance, legal, and IT services. Weske's (2010) multilevel characterization, from organizational strategy to implemented business processes, supports this view. Figure 4.3 shows the conceptual business process hierarchy hereof.

The figure shows a *hierarchical* flow between process levels, either downstream or upstream. The sequentially focused process levels are identified as follows:

- Organizational strategies: These define the organization's long-term objectives, such as becoming the cost-efficiency leader in the industry in our context.
- Organizational goals: Operational goals and subgoals are developed based on the defined strategies, such as increasing production efficiency or finding alternative raw-material suppliers.
- Organizational business processes: These are characterized by granular business processes resulting from multiple operational processes. Organizational business processes include the flow of cost information between the finance function, other organizational functions, and various functions within the finance function.
- Operational business processes: These specify activities and relationships. Cost management systems design, for example, describes cost calculations and logical information flow between business functions.

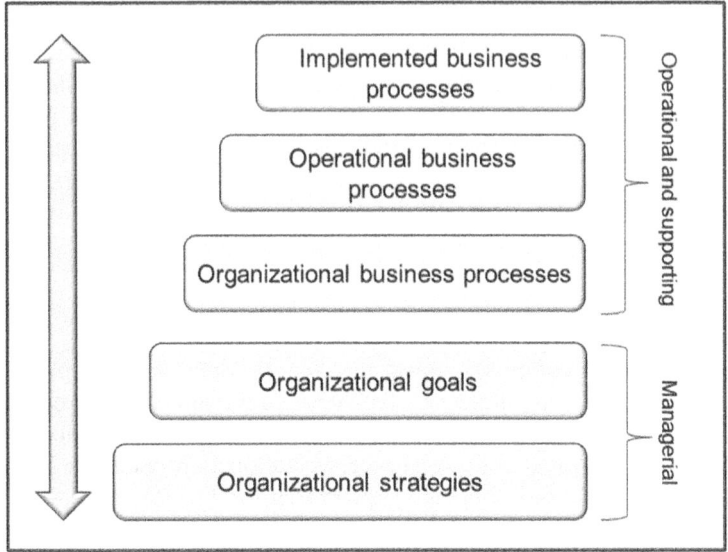

**Fig. 4.3** Business process hierarchy

- Implemented business processes: This level concerns information about executing process activities and the organizational and technical environments in which they occur. For managerial costing systems, this includes hardware and software requirements.

Typical business process analysis and modeling are often initially focused on internal operations. However, the *Fourth Industrial Revolution* has expanded such possibilities, allowing business process management to extend beyond organizational boundaries.

### 4.2.4    Business Process Life Cycle

The concept of a business process life cycle involving the creation, management, and conclusion of business processes is crucial for effective process management. This life cycle consists of interrelated phases, usually organized in a cyclical structure, as depicted in Fig. 4.4.

As shown in the figure, the activities of the life cycle consider critical stakeholders (role-players) at all levels *Internal* stakeholders often have

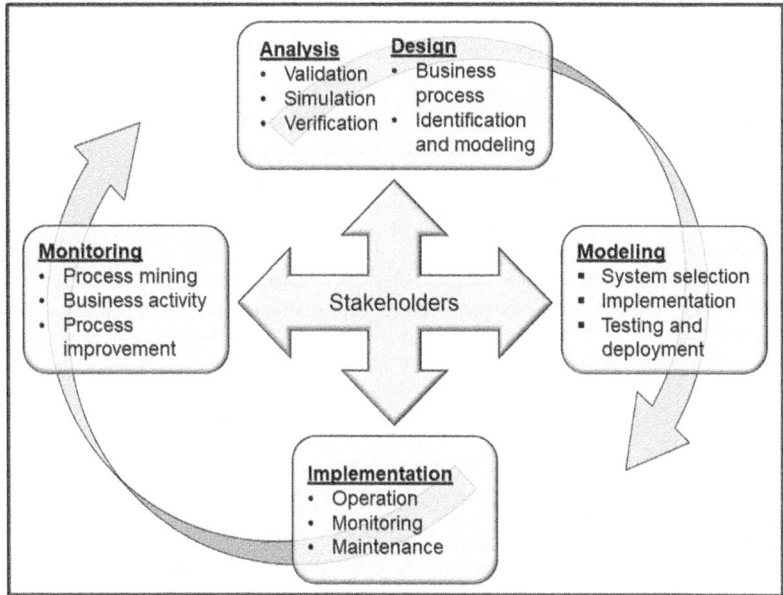

**Fig. 4.4**  Conceptual business process life cycle

the necessary knowledge about and experience of the process instance and actively participate in the organization's process activities, whereas *external* stakeholders, beyond the organization and process activities, may also play a role as providers in and beneficiaries of various processes and deliverables (Aldin and De Cesare 2011; Hnatkowska and Cebinka 2021).

The life cycle activities may include the following:

- Analysis and design: This initial phase in the life cycle focuses on the organizational and technical aspects of the business process instance. It involves developing an initial process model that undergoes validation, simulation, and verification.
- Modeling: In this phase, the business process system is configured based on the organizational environment. The system is then implemented, tested, and deployed if all requirements are met.

- Implementation: During this phase, the process is enacted, and monitoring, maintenance, and testing are conducted to ensure that it meets the necessary goals and requirements.
- Monitoring: The final phase evaluates the process model using available information. Possible improvement areas may be identified, leading to potential process redesign and reanalysis.

The typical business process life cycle is in a state of continuous improvement, leading to the development of process improvement philosophies. Key aspects of the business improvement concept are explained in the next section.

### 4.2.5    Business Process Improvement

Although this book's focus is not primarily on process improvement, an overview of well-known operational improvement methodologies is essential, since they are integral to process mapping and analysis objectives. Additionally, operations-centric costing methodologies discussed in Chapter Five can support and complement process improvement initiatives. Malinova and Mendling (2021) opine that process models support business improvement efforts, and Hnatkowska and Cebinka (2021) concur that process modeling, through textual specifications and graphical presentations, can highlight quality issues in context.

Despite their separate development contexts, the following examples often share philosophical alignment with the process improvement concept:

- Lean manufacturing: Lean is a manufacturing philosophy aiming to minimize production times, materials, and efforts (Hassan and Kajiwara 2013). It is part of a process improvement mindset, aligned with approaches such as business process reengineering (Shah et al. 2008), focused on waste elimination and value-adding activities (Ahmad and Soberi 2018). Thus, lean principles encourage effectiveness and efficiency, reducing waste activities in the value stream (Krogstie 2016). These principles include identifying customers and value, mapping the value stream, creating improved flow, responding to customer requirements, and pursuing perfection. The concept of Kaizen adds the dimension of continuous improvement through more minor incremental changes (Kumar et al. 2018). Building close relationships with supply chain participants is also highlighted in the lean manufacturing philosophy (Van Assen 2021). Just-in-time (JIT) and total quality management (TQM) are considered subsystems of the lean philosophy.

- Just-in-time: Toyota pioneered JIT in the early 1970s as part of the Toyota Production System, which aims to eliminate waste and inefficiency in order to enhance efficiency in production processes and optimize the supply chain (PourAsiabi and PourAsiabi 2012). JIT operates as a *pull system*, where items are produced based on subsequent production activity requirements,[1] thus eliminating excess inventory and initiating production activities based on customer or workstation requests (Hassan and Kajiwara 2013). The Kanban system within a typical JIT environment manages inventory control and signaling functions (Braglia et al. 2020; Khojasteh and Sato 2015). This approach of minimal or zero inventory quickly reveals flaws and issues in the value chain, demanding a stable and reliable supply chain, in which defects are not tolerated, as they can disrupt the entire production process.

- Total quality management: This is a management philosophy that focuses on continuously improving product, service, and people quality to achieve customer satisfaction (Al-Shourah and Al-Shourah 2020; Talib and Faisal 2020). It involves customer-oriented practices, integrated management, strategic thinking, increased employee involvement, close customer and supplier relationships, and cost-of-quality monitoring (Nguyen and Nagase 2019; Marchiori and Mendes 2020). TQM principles have been found to enhance operational and business performance, leading to product enhancement by reducing nonvalue-adding activities, time, and costs (Tarí and García-Fernández 2020). TQM also promotes incremental or radical innovation in both business processes and products, thus fostering continual detection, reduction, and elimination of manufacturing errors and inefficiencies and in turn streamlining the supply chain and improving customer experiences.

- Six Sigma: Six Sigma has similar philosophies and objectives to TQM, and has been described as 'TQM on steroids' (Farahbod

---

[1] This stands in contrast to the *push system* in which items are manufactured and stored in inventory, rather than based of actual subsequent production requirements.

et al. 2022) and is a set of techniques for process improvement aligned with organizational goals (Ishak et al. 2022). It aims to enhance product and service quality by identifying and eliminating defects, reducing business process variability, and improving manufacturing efficiencies (Ekleş and Türkmen 2022). Unlike TQM, however, Six Sigma targets the center of tolerance levels and does not tolerate any deviation. Six Sigma employs empirical and statistical quality management techniques, following defined methodologies with specific value targets, such as reducing waste or increasing customer satisfaction (Efimova et al. 2021). It typically uses two methodologies, namely DMAIC (define, measure, analyze, improve, and control) for reactive process improvement and DMADV (define, measure, analyze, design, and verify) for proactive product or process development.

Many of the mentioned methodologies highlight their contribution to customer satisfaction, supporting the idea that core business processes revolve around it. Van Assen (2021), however, found that organizations often fail to implement such programs, citing the unique characteristics and operations within each organization as the reason. Instead of implementing improvement *programs*, organizations should adopt an improvement *philosophy*. Tailoring the design of managerial costing systems to each context can contribute hereto and increase the likelihood of success.

## 4.3    BUSINESS PROCESS MANAGEMENT

The next focus will be on specific business process management (BPM) concepts, delving into two key supporting areas: business process reengineering and model abstraction.

### 4.3.1    *Business Process Reengineering*

BPM has its roots in scientific management principles, evolving through concepts such as lean, JIT, TQM, Six Sigma, and business process reengineering (BPR) (Fragoso 2015). Early on, Hammer and Champy (1993) described BPR as fundamentally rethinking and redesigning business processes to improve performance measures. Contemporary authors such as Virzi (2019) suggest that effective BPR can significantly upgrade organizations and contribute to performance and innovation. Fragoso (2015) emphasizes BPR involvement in combining various related techniques and concepts. We can therefore view BPR as a design philosophy without specific execution guidelines, that can contribute to the evolution of BPM.

There are two perspectives on BPM; it is regarded as (i) a general management principle for sustaining competitive advantage and (ii) a methodological perspective defined by methods and techniques of analysis, improvement, design, and control of business processes. Hyötyläinen (2015) links BPM to the topic of this book, considering BPM systems as open, cybernetic nilpotent systems that require external stimuli to change a stable system into an agitated state (goal-driven quest) before returning to stability. We therefore accept that BPM goes beyond mere technical applications and acknowledge the need to apply relevant techniques to design process models effectively.

Therefore, BPM is viewed as a management discipline focused on improving organizational performance through analyzing, monitoring, and changing processes for greater effectiveness and efficiency. It also contributes to the organization's ability to create economic value.

### 4.3.2 Model Abstraction

A *business model* is an abstraction of a business's operations, whereas a *business process model* focuses on the organization's behavior (Aldin and De Cesare 2011). Similarly, mapping from a domain of interest to a diagram is an abstraction or decomposition (Malinova and Mendling 2021. Abstraction denotes complex system components and organizational relations (Kuokkanen 2022; Hnatkowska and Cebinka 2021). Though traditionally used in software design and IT, abstraction can also help conceptualize a process model for designing managerial costing systems. Figure 4.5 illustrates various abstraction dimensions available for capturing the complexity of managing business processes.

Contextually illustrated in the figure, the abstraction dimensions are explained as follows:

- Vertical abstraction: This dimension considers subdomains within the organization's context (Kuokkanen 2022). Vertical abstraction is used when subdomains need separate representation and analysis,

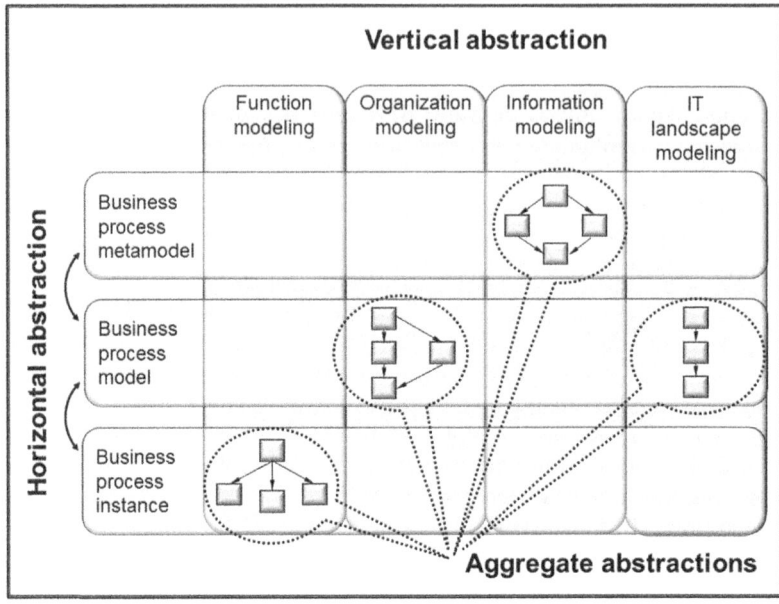

**Fig. 4.5** Primary abstraction dimensions

for example (i) function modeling, focusing on work in the business process context; (ii) organization modeling, accurately representing the organizational structures to identify interfaces between operational and functional areas; (iii) information modeling, addressing data requirements and dependencies between functions and activities; and (iv) IT landscape modeling, reflecting the technological link between business functions, business processes, and the generating of management information.

- Horizontal abstraction: Horizontal abstraction focuses on a specific level within the organization (Kuokkanen 2022), and in this regard, we can differentiate several hierarchical levels, including (i) the business process instance level (user object layer) that deals with activities, data values, and resources in the business process context; (ii) the business process model level, which categorizes and represents sets of similar process instances; (iii) the business process metamodel level, which focuses on relationships and connections between business process models; and (iv) multiple metalevels, which can be applied conceptually based on the scenario and business complexity. The metamodel describes process model (s), which describes process instance(s). Conversely, the process instance level(s) reflects instances within the process model, reflecting instances within the metamodel.

• Aggregate abstraction: Krogstie (2016) introduces aggregate abstraction as an additional dimension. It deepens horizontal abstraction by aggregating business functions at the instance level within a specific vertical subdomain.

Business objectives are dynamic, and processes change over time, leading to potential changes and transformations in process models, including abstraction levels. Such business transformations are often defined at the metamodel level, where model-to-model transformations occur (Hnatkowska and Cebinka 2021). When designing managerial costing systems as part of strategic and economic value creation objectives, ensuring the appropriate abstraction for a specific business level is crucial.

## 4.4    Business Process Modeling

Business process models are the critical conceptual artifacts for updating business processes and contributing to value creation. The following sections will focus on the modeling aspects.

### 4.4.1    From the Value System to the Business Process

Krogstie (2016) mentions that *Fourth Industrial Revolution* technologies enhance BPM applications, increasing the efficiency and effectiveness of business processes across value chains. Mapping of the physical organization of the business operation is essential as a foundation for modeling business operations. This map should be based on operational functions and differs from an organizational chart. Kumar et al. (2018) suggest that continuous improvements can be achieved through process mapping, visualizing waste, and triggering process improvement activities. Aldin and De Cesare (2011) opine that emphasizing the importance of an integrated process view cuts across functional boundaries, surpassing the traditional functional view.

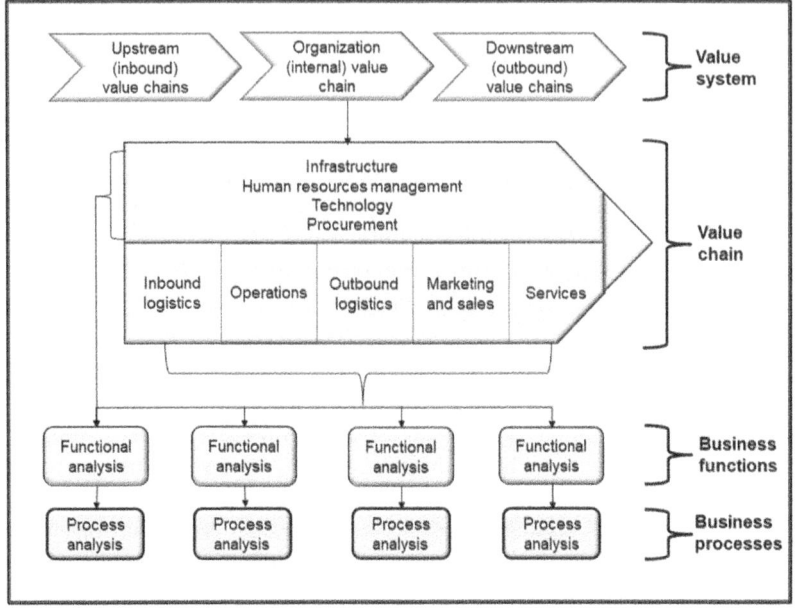

**Fig. 4.6** Functional decomposition (*Source* Adapted from Porter 1985)

For the purposes of this book, we assert that organizational value chains, as the foundational basis, offer a high-level overview of organizational functions, which can be further analyzed into granular business functions and processes for a detailed view. Figure 4.6 illustrates such a contextual overview.

The figure conceptually illustrates the *value system* as the highest level of aggregation, encompassing the organization's inbound and outbound value chains. Within this context is the internal *value chain(s)*, each with its own value chain component(s), involving various *business functions*, including function-specific *business processes* or activities.

### 4.4.2   Modeling Approaches

Malinova and Mendling (2021) emphasize the importance of the modeling concept in systems analysis and design. Process modeling efforts should identify the main concepts of the process to be represented

(Aldin and De Cesare 2011). The model's sophistication should align with the organization's operations, business environment, and strategic goals to provide the required level of decision support (Lawson et al. 2019). A process map (Ahmad and Soberi 2018) or process model (Weske 2010) serves as a blueprint for a set of process instances and helps model designers understand the dynamic and static aspects of the system (Malinova and Mendling 2021). In designing managerial costing systems, flowcharting of the organizational processes and resources is crucial to ensure effective analysis of complex operations. These flowcharts also assist in identifying critical success factors and relevant cost metrics within the specific context.

Business process modeling should begin by considering three typical goals: (i) understanding the process's functioning; (ii) illustrating the process to others; and (iii) analyzing the process for potential improvements. We can distinguish several critical process components that need to be modeled, including (i) the critical process components to be modeled; (ii) the process itself, consisting of activities, outcomes (goals), and anticipated outputs (products and services); (iii) the sequence of activities in the process; (iv) the events occurring during the process, such as starting, intermediate, and ending events; (v) decisions made during the process, referred to as gateways; (vi) roles within the process; (vii) data objects and information requirements and generation within the process; and (viii) physical objects involved in the process.

Several techniques are available for modeling, and the use of diagrams in systems analysis and design has been extensively researched, with their advantages over conventional textual descriptions well documented, such as improved systematic refinement and verifiability (Bunse 2006), enhanced comprehension of source code (Dzidek et al. 2008), better judgment of functional requirements (Schlauderer and Overhage 2018), and more effective elicitation of requirements (Trkman et al. 2016). In context, Hnatkowska and Cebinka (2021) opine that textual element formats would typically benefit nontechnical users, while diagrams help technical users and developers. Therefore, graphical representations arguably facilitate accessibility of analysis and identification of inefficiencies and inconsistencies compared with textual specifications. Three frequently used, basic techniques are highlighted here for illustrative purposes in context:

- Swimlane flowcharts: As the most basic approach, the swimlane concept enables the clear assignment of tasks to role-players and activities (Killich et al. 1999). Figure 4.7 shows a typical example of a swimlane flowchart.
  Figure 4.7 indicates that, although swimlane flowcharts typically show the activities, decisions, and roles within the business process, they often do not provide much information about events, data objects, and physical objects. As such, although swimlane flowcharts offer a simple representation for understanding process overviews (often for nontechnical stakeholders), they may provide only limited opportunity for proper process analysis.
- Unified Modeling Language (UML) activity diagrams: Extending the sophistication of the swimlane concept is the UML, which, according to Sornkliang and Phetkaew (2021), is an activity diagram flowchart that chronologically organizes the events (activities) that take place within a process. Even though the UML activity diagram

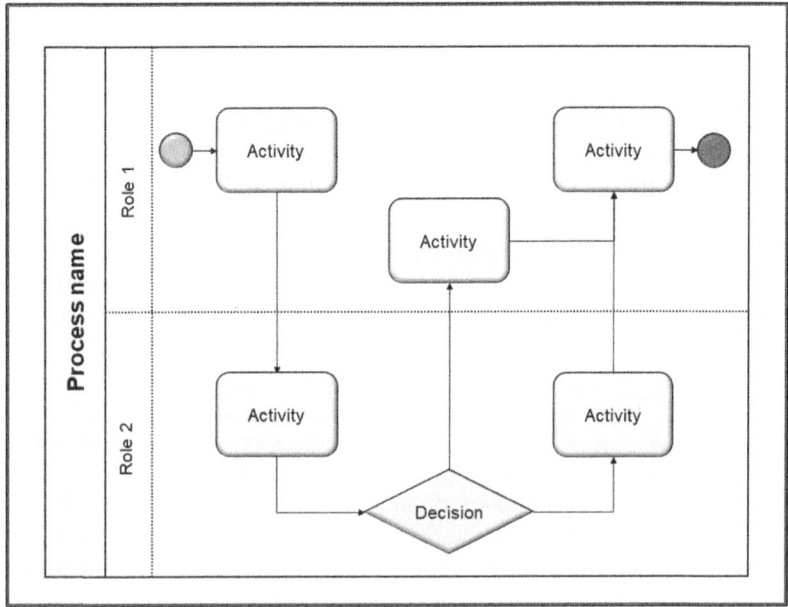

**Fig. 4.7**  Illustration of a swimlane flowchart

approach was designed as a standard specification for IT-related architecture, it has some value for business process modeling. Figure 4.8 shows an example of a UML activity diagram.

Like the swimlane approach, in some contexts, a UML activity diagram addresses the criterion of indicating the activities, events, decisions, roles, data objectives, and requirements within the business process. However, Aldin and De Cesare (2011) opine that it is limited in providing explicit information regarding business processes, and Killich et al. (1999) point out that UML focuses on (object-orientated) software design rather than work system design. Therefore, although UML activity diagrams facilitate the understanding and analysis of business processes, they tend to favor the stakeholders with higher levels of UML expertise.

- Business Process Model and Notation (BPMN) diagrams: According to Krogstie (2016), the BPMN approach was specifically developed to provide a notation understandable to the relevant business users.

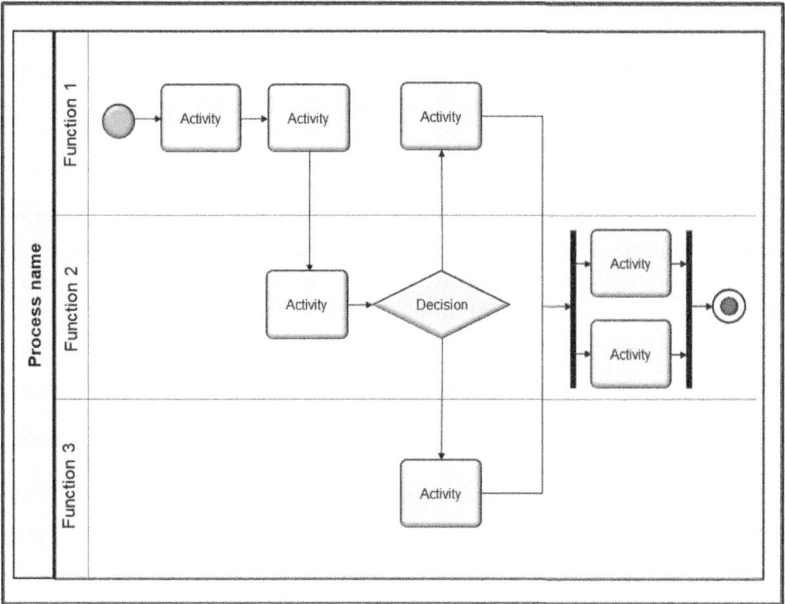

**Fig. 4.8** Illustration of a UML activity diagram

It is successful herein because it includes verbal and visual elements (Malinova and Mendling 2021). It is not primarily focused on IT-related process mapping, i.e., for functional technical specialists, but also serves to empower the businesspeople who need to manage the processes. The following component categories are typical examples found in the BPMN toolset:

- Functional grouping components hold the various process components together: (i) The *pools* indicate separate external (public) business processes, which depict the interaction between multiple organizations, or indicate internal (private) business processes, which depict processes specific to the organization. (ii) The *swimlanes* act as graphical containers for a set of activities, indicating the functional breakdown and organizational subsets.
- Flow components encompass the shapes inside: (i) The *activities* denote the work done within the process. (ii) The *decisions* (or gateways) indicate a branching or merging of process paths and include exclusive or parallel gateways. (iii) The *events* identify the things that happen in the process and are either starting, intermediate, or ending events. (iv) The *connecting components* link the flow objects and distinguish between sequential flows, message flows, and associations.
- Artifacts are the data objects, groups, and annotations.

Figure 4.9 provides a basic illustration of a process model using BPMN.

According to Malinova and Mendling (2021), each symbol in the diagram would contain a *term* describing the events, decisions, choices, etc., and the language of textual elements would inherit their semantics from natural language. Furthermore, the ideograms used can also often be associated with concrete images.

## 4.5    Chapter Summary

This chapter has discussed the role of business processes in designing managerial costing systems, covering process modeling, levels, classification, life cycle, and improvements. The relevance of BPM, BPR and related concepts, and model abstraction was touched upon, along with value systems analysis and technical modeling approaches. The upcoming

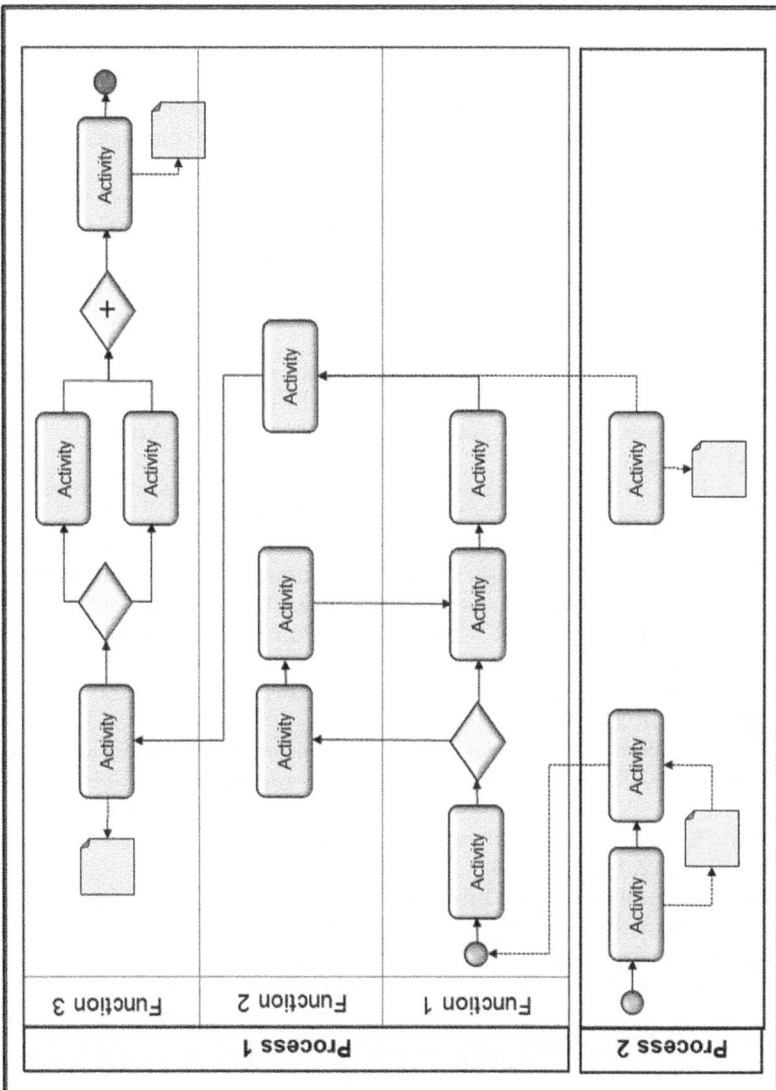

Fig. 4.9 Illustration of a BPMN process model

chapter will delve into the complexities of cost accounting within the framework of developing the managerial costing system.

## REFERENCES

Ahmad, R. and Soberi, M.S.F. 2018. Changeover process improvement based on modified SMED method and other process improvement tools application: an improvement project of 5-axis CNC machine operation in advanced composite manufacturing industry. *The International Journal of Advanced Manufacturing Technology*, 94:433–450. https://doi.org/10.1007/s00170-017-0827-7.

Aldin, L. and De Cesare, S. 2011. A literature review on business process modelling: New frontiers of reusability. *Enterprise Information Systems*, 5(3):359–383.

Al-Shourah, S. and Al-Shourah, A.A. 2020. An examination between total quality management and hotel financial performance: Evidence from Jordanian international hotels. *Journal of Management Information and Decision Sciences*, 23(1):418–431.

Bhaskar, H.L. 2018. Business process reengineering: A process based management tool. *Serbian Journal of Management*, 13(1):63–87.

Braglia, M., Gabbrielli, R. and Marrazzini, L. 2020, Rolling Kanban: a new visual tool to schedule family batch manufacturing processes with Kanban. *International Journal of Production Research*, 58(13):3998–4014.

Bronzo, M., de Resende, P.T.V., de Oliviera, M.P.V., McCormack, K.P., de Sousa, P.R. and Ferreira, R.L. 2013. Improving performance aligning business analytics with process orientation. *International Journal of Information Management*, 33:300–307.

Bunse, C. 2006. Using patterns for the refinement and translation of UML models: A controlled experiment. *Empirical Software Engineering*, 11(2):227–267.

Duckert, G.H. 2011. *Practical enterprise risk management*. New Jersey: Wiley Corporate F&A. 275p.

Dzidek, W.J., Arisholm, E. and Briand, L.C. 2008. A realistic empirical evaluation of the costs and benefits of UML in software maintenance. *IEEE Transactions on Software Engineering*, 34(3):407–432.

Efimova, A., Bris, P. and Efimov, A. 2021. A bibliometric analysis of the evolution of Six Sigma in the context of industry 4.0. *Inzinerine Ekonomika-Engineering Economics*, 32(4):338–349. https://doi.org/10.5755/j01.ee.32.4.28536.

Ekleş, E. and Türkmen, M.A. 2022. Integrating the theory of constraints and Six Sigma: Process improvement implementation. *Istanbul Business Research*, 51(1):123–147. https://doi.org/10.26650/ibr.2022.51.938481.

Farahbod, K., Shayo, C. and Varzandeh, J. 2022. Six Sigma and Lean operations in cybersecurity management. *Journal of Business and Behavioral Sciences*, 34(1):99–109.

Fragoso, J.T. 2015. Business process reengineering in government agencies: Lessons from an experience in Mexico. *Journal of Service Science and Management*, 8(3):382–392.

Hammer, M. and Champy, J. 1993. *Reengineering the corporation: A manifesto for business revolution*. New York, NY: Harper Business Press.

Hassan, K. and Kajiwara, H. 2013. Application of pull concept-based lean production system in the ship building industry. *Journal of Ship Production and Design*, 29(3):105–116. https://doi.org/10.5957/JSPD.29.3.120021.

Hnatkowska, B. and Cebinka, M. 2021. Activity diagram generation based on use-case textual specification. *Computing and Informatics*, 40:772–795. https://doi.org/10.31577/cai_2021_4_772.

Hyötyläinen, T. 2015. *Steps to improve firm performance with business process management*. Springer Gabler. https://doi.org/10.1007/978-3-658-074 70-8.

Ishak, A.B., Mohamad, E.B. and Arep, H.B.A. 2022. The application of Six Sigma for process control analysis in the Malaysian poultry wastewater treatment. *Journal of Ecological Engineering*, 23(5):116–129. https://doi.org/10. 12911/22998993/147273.

Khojasteh, Y. and Sato, R. 2015. Selection of a pull production control system in multi-stage production processes. *International Journal of Production Research*, 53(140): 4363–4379. https://doi.org/10.1080/00207543.2014. 1001530.

Killich, S., Luczak, H., Schlick, C., Weissenbach, M., Wiedenmaier, S. and Ziegler, J. 1999. Task modelling for cooperative work. *Behaviour and Information Technology*, 18(5):325–338.

Krogstie, J. 2016. *Quality in business process modelling*. Springer Cham. https://doi.org/10.1007/978-3-319-42512-2.

Kumar, S., Dhingra, A.K. and Singh, B. 2018. Process improvement through Lean-Kaizen using value stream map: A case study in India. *The International Journal of Advanced Manufacturing Technology*, 96:2687–2698. https://doi.org/10.1007/s00170-018-1684-8.

Kuokkanen, J. 2022. Vertical-horizontal distinction in resolving the abstraction, hierarchy, and generality problems of the mechanistic account of physical computation. *Synthese*, 200:247. https://doi.org/10.1007/s11229-022-037 25-8.

Lawson, R., Cokins, G., Hicks, D.T., Krumwiede, K., Swain, M. and White, L. 2019. Costing system attributes that support good decision making. Statements on Management Accounting. Institute of Management Accountants (IMA), Montvale, N.J.

Malinova, M. and Mendling, J. 2021. Cognitive diagram understanding and task performance in systems analysis and design. *MIS Quarterly*, 45(4):2101–2157. https://doi.org/10.25300/MISQ/2021/15262.

Marchiori, D. and Mendes, L. 2020. Knowledge management and total quality management: foundations, intellectual structures, insights regarding evolution of the literature. *Total Quality Management*, 31(10):1135–1169. https://doi.org/10.1080/14783363.2018.1468247.

Nguyen, T.L.H. and Nagase, K. 2019. The influence of total quality management on customer satisfaction. *International Journal of Healthcare Management*, 12(4):277–285. https://doi.org/10.1080/20479700.2019.1647378.

Porter, M.E. 1985. *Competitive advantage: Creating and sustaining superior performance*. New York: Simon and Schuster.

PourAsiabi, H. and PourAsiabi, H. 2012. Just in time (JIT) production and supply chain management. International Iron & Steel Symposium, 02–04 April 2012, Karabük, Türkiye.

Schlauderer, S. and Overhage, S. 2018. BOSDL: An approach to describe the business logic of software services in domain-specific terms. *Business & Information Systems Engineering*, 60(5):393–413.

Shah, R., Chandrasekaran, A. and Linderman, K. 2008. In pursuit of implementation patterns: The context of Lean and Six Sigma. *International Journal of Production Research*, 46(23):6679–6699. https://doi.org/10.1080/00207540802230504.

Sornkliang, W. and Phetkaew, T. 2021. Target-based test path prioritization for UML activity diagram using weight assignment methods. *International Journal of Electrical and Computer Engineering*, 11(1):575–588. https://doi.org/10.11591/ijece.v11i1.pp575-588.

Talib, F. and Faisal, M.N. 2020. Assessment of total quality management implementation in Indian service industries. *The IUP Journal of Operations Management*, 19(2):7–28.

Tarhan, A., Turetken, O. and Reijers, H.A. 2016. Business process maturity models: A systematic literature review. *Information and Software Technology*, 75:122–134.

Tarí, J.J. and García-Fernández, M. 2020. A proposal for a scale measuring innovation in a total quality management context. *Total Quality Management*, 31(15):1703–1717. https://doi.org/10.1080/14783363.2018.1504622.

Trkman, M., Mendling, J. and Krisper, M. 2016. Using business process models to better understand the dependencies among user stories. *Information and Software Technology*, 71: 58–76.

Van Assen, M.F. 2021. Lean, process improvement and customer-focused performance. The moderating effect of perceived organisational context. *Total Quality Management*, 32(1):57–75. https://doi.org/10.1080/14783363.2018.1530591.

Virzi, K. 2019. Examining the success and failure factors of business process reengineering in Africa, Asia, the Middle East, and North America: A literature review. *Open Access Library Journal*, 6:e5722. https://doi.org/10.4236/oalib.1105722.

Weske, M. 2010. *Business process management: Concepts, languages, architectures.* Berlin: Springer-Verlag. p. 368.

# CHAPTER 5

# Cost Accounting Perspectives

The preceding chapter offered insights into business processes and their relevance to this book. This chapter delves deeper into the book's literature foundation, specifically exploring the complexities of cost accounting and the wide range of available approaches and methods.

## 5.1   Background

Drury (2015) claims that effective cost management is necessitated by the impact of organizational development on accounting policies. This assertion is supported by Go and Weng (2021), who acknowledge the critical role of costing approaches, methods, and systems in organizational management. Zhang and Liu (2020) emphasize the importance of cost optimization and control in gaining a competitive edge, while Novák et al. (2017) underline the significance of cost management in operational and financial performance. Finally, Raef et al. (2019a) distinguish between the historical focus of cost accounting and the forward-looking cost management approach. In modern times, understanding costs remains crucial for supporting effective operational decision-making and price determination, as evidenced by Banker et al. (2018) and Li et al. (2021).

In light of the above, we emphasize that effective cost management extends beyond *cost reduction* alone. It necessitates prioritizing resource

P. W. Buys, *Crafting Efficiency in Managerial Costing System Design*, https://doi.org/10.1007/978-981-97-0934-2_5

optimization and enhancing production efficiency. Understanding cost-related concepts while creating the envisioned process model will provide valuable insights for a managerial costing framework.

## 5.2   Production Environment

Prior to designing the desired managerial costing system, careful consideration of the production environment in which it will operate is crucial. The production environment will determine the appropriate costing system, be it job costing, process costing, or a *hybrid* costing system.

### 5.2.1   *Job Costing*

In a job costing production environment, all associated costs are allocated to individual products or batches, and this method is applicable when there is an identifiable distinct cost object unit (Yegínboy and Y"uksel 2015). Job costing is, therefore, suitable for unique or limited edition products, such as bespoke items for specific clients like buildings, factories, yachts, or custom vehicles. It involves accumulating direct costs (materials and labor) and indirect costs (manufacturing overhead) for each job and tracing specific costs to individual assignments. Figure 5.1 provides an overview of cost flows in this environment.

As per Alami and ElMaraghy's (2020) findings, job costing typically comprises the following steps: (i) Defining the specific product and gathering its associated costs on separate cost sheets; (ii) identifying the direct costs (material and labor) related to the product; (iii) determining the manufacturing overhead (indirect costs) associated with the product and selecting a cost allocation method; (iv) calculating the indirect cost rate per unit and allocating indirect costs to the product; and lastly (v) determining the total job costs (or product) by combining direct and indirect costs.

### 5.2.2   *Process Costing*

A process costing production environment, as described by Alami and ElMaraghy (2020), is appropriate for continuously manufacturing identical products, such as chemical refineries, vehicle production lines, and food processing. This system gathers direct material, labor, and manufacturing overhead costs for each production department and assigns them

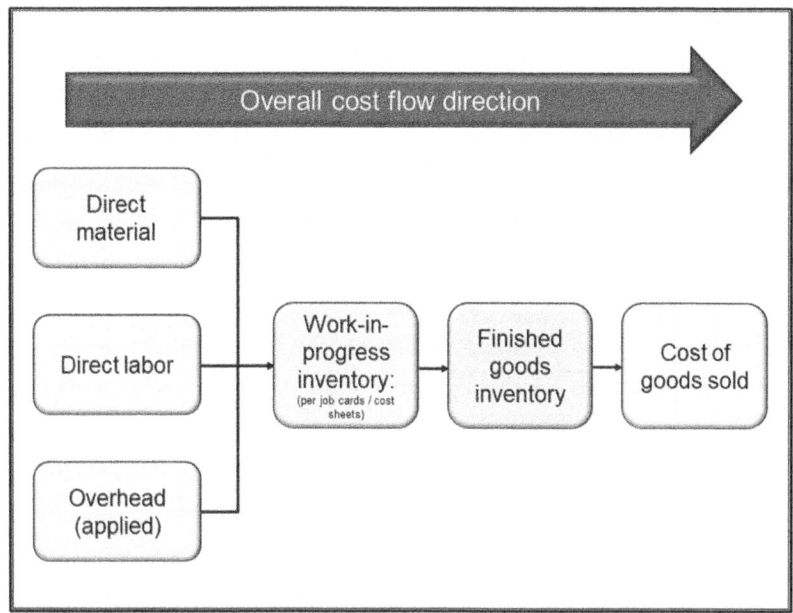

**Fig. 5.1** Cost flow overview: job costing

to *equivalent* product units, representing the proportionate completed units. Figure 5.2 illustrates an overview of the cost flows in this setting.

As per the findings of Alami and ElMaraghy (2020), process costing generally encompasses the following steps: (i) Summarizing the flow of physical units throughout the production value chain; (ii) computing equivalent unit outputs based on the quantity of each input (both completed and in progress), and converting this quantity to the number of units that could have been completed given the resources used; (iii) summarizing the overall costs, inclusive of direct material costs and conversion costs (encompassing direct labor and manufacturing overhead); (iv) calculating the cost per equivalent unit; and (v) allocating total costs to both completed units and units that are in work-in-progress.

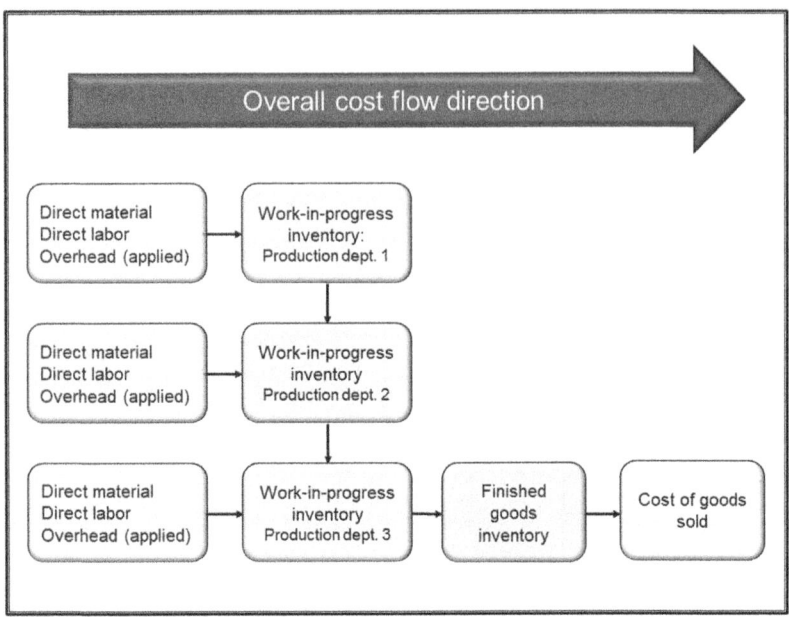

**Fig. 5.2** Cost flow overview: process costing

### 5.2.3 Operational Costing

In spite of variances in their application contexts, both job costing and process costing share a common objective: to approximate the costs associated with producing goods. Operational *costing* represents a hybrid approach (Lewis, n.d.), amalgamating components from both job and process costing (Krumwiede and Walden 2013). In the realm of job costing, expenses are meticulously monitored across each phase of production, whereas within process costing, expenditures are aggregated per department prior to transitioning to the subsequent stage. Fundamentally, operational costing mirrors process costing, though it might include items with minor divergences in materials or quality (Lewis, n.d.), such as a production line crafting computers with varying specifications. However, in contrast to process costing, which computes the cost per equivalent unit for work-in-progress, operational costing strives to minimize work-in-progress inventory at the conclusion of each production cycle.

## 5.3  Costing Concepts

Although grasping the intricacies of costs and associated principles is crucial when designing managerial costing systems, it may prove to be more challenging than it sounds. On one side, Go and Weng (2021) distinguish between *cost* and *value*, asserting that value is a more comprehensive notion, including costs and their resultant benefits. Conversely, Labro (2019) regards costs as intangible and abstract, signifying an economically valuable resource. Particularly pertinent to our context are perspectives that highlight costs as a gauge of the influence of managerial actions, extending beyond mere resource consumption. Contemporary research in cost management suggests that costs are steered by managers (Banker et al. 2018), thereby making cost management centered around overseeing organizational activities that give rise to cost accrual.

The concept of "cost" pertains to the exertion needed to create and distribute a product. However, given that numerous costs hinge on presumed allocation rates, contention arises that *true* costs are elusive, and instead, we deal with *estimated* costs. To fully comprehend its influence on organizational performance and decision-making, one must consider the behavioral and managerial implications of the cost concept on crucial management endeavors.

### 5.3.1  Cost Behavior

Özçelik (2019) suggests that contemporary organizations struggle with sustaining profitability in an environment characterized by elevated fixed costs. A comprehensive understanding of cost behavior and classification dynamics is crucial in furnishing management with the means to uphold or reestablish profitability. The exploration of cost behavior, an extensively researched subject within academic and industrial domains (Banker et al. 2018; Li et al. 2021), highlights the interplay between business operations and cost accrual. Precise cost classification is crucial in facilitating meticulous cost analysis (Novák et al. 2017), while a profound grasp of cost behavior is essential in managerial decision-making (Magheed 2016). Hence, an awareness of how costs change in tandem with levels of activity emerges as a critical linchpin for the exercise of management control and the formulation of financial and operational plans. Within this paradigm, certain costs fluctuate in response to operational activities, while others maintain autonomy, thereby giving rise to the dichotomy of fixed and variable costs.

- Fixed vs. variable costs: Fixed costs (FC) are generally not directly tied to operational activities and exhibit constancy within specific levels of activity (Hultman 2021). They are typically represented as a horizontal line intersecting the vertical cost axis at the monetary value equivalent of FC. In contrast, variable costs (VC) correlate directly with activity levels (Hultman 2021) and could be viewed as a consistent cost per output unit. These distinctions are illustrated in Fig. 5.3.

  As indicated in Fig. 5.3, the FC curve originates from the cost axis, denoting a baseline cost in the absence of operational activity. Conceptually, the VC curve commences at the point of zero-cost

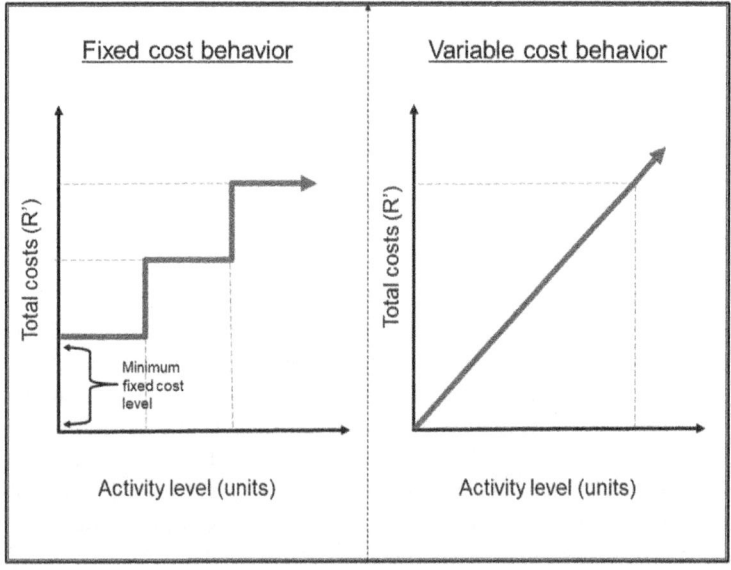

**Fig. 5.3** Fixed vs. variable cost behavior

intersection, representing the absence of variable costs when operational activities are at a minimum (for example, no units produced or labor hours utilized). Mathematically, the total cost associated with a given level of operational activity result from the combination of FC and VC and is expressed as follows:

$$\text{Total cost} = \text{FC} + \left( \text{VC rate} \times \text{output units} \right)$$

Although the *traditional* cost behavior model is conceptually sound, it is acknowledged that costs generally do not fall strictly under fixed or variable categories (Novák et al. 2017). Nonetheless, for accurate cost classification, it is imperative to understand the output linked with operations and discern the fundamental activities and the reasons behind shifts at the operational level.

• Sticky costs: The conventional cost classifications mentioned earlier assume a direct correlation between cost fluctuations and activity levels. However, various studies conducted by Magheed (2016), Bradbury and Scott (2018), Da Silva et al. (2019), Hosomi and Nagasawa (2018), and Reynoso et al. (2021) have highlighted that costs often deviate from this proportional response to changes in activity levels. This phenomenon, known as cost stickiness, introduces complexity to predicting and estimating future costs. Cost stickiness stems from a range of internal factors, such as administrative decisions, technology, employment, debt, production capacity, assets, and cost structures, and external factors, such as industry attributes, demand uncertainties, economic conditions, and legislative and social security considerations. While existing literature often employs examples of comprehensive selling and administrative costs to illustrate this phenomenon, it is important to acknowledge the relevance of sticky cost behavior when designing a managerial costing system. Such behavior could be influenced by production capacity, asset utilization, and internal cost structures, including allocating support department costs to production departments.

Understanding cost behavior holds paramount importance for the efficient management of operations. Focusing on the repercussions of choices, a perspective akin to a *black-box* unveils the nature of cost behavior, thereby enabling a comprehensive assessment of the intricate interplay between management decisions and other components within the organizational framework. It is imperative to acknowledge that all costs are variable over an extended time frame under the influence of managerial judgment. Hence, the management of costs ought to pivot around the events or catalysts that instigate such changes.

### 5.3.2   Managerial Considerations

Achieving managerial objectives necessitates the generation of outcomes, a process contingent upon utilizing available resources (Raef et al. 2019b). Effective resource allocation demands adept cost control, as highlighted by Bozkurt et al. (2014), encompassing a spectrum of cost concepts that extend beyond fiscal factors. Within the context of cost management, two significant ideas emerge, as highlighted in the following discussion:

- Control: A manager's influence over a particular cost item varies based on the circumstances. Costs are classified as controllable when a manager can approve them within a given period (Horngren et al. 2015). In a given context, associated direct costs could be readily linked to a specific product, allowing the ability to decide whether to produce it. In contrast, indirect costs, which lack a direct connection to a product and are often associated with assisted supportive services and fixed period costs, might accrue and are subject to less manageable oversight (Novák et al. 2017; Togha et al. 2021). Hence, effective managerial control encompasses both the monetary aspect and the circumstances leading to specific cost accrual.
- Planning: Several pertinent cost concepts play a role in this given context. The notion of *relevant* costs pertains to specific situations, aiding in decisions tailored to each case. These costs typically encompass future expenses that choices could influence (Hultman 2021). In contrast, *differential* costs differ between available options and embody costs that could be avoided by choosing one option over another (Sicuro Corrêa et al. 2018). *Opportunity* costs reflect the potential benefits foregone when opting for one alternative over another: They signify the missed profit resulting from changes in input factors (Cooper and Stoner 2021). Finally, *sunk* costs refer to historical expenses that have already been incurred and remain constant regardless of present or future decisions (Sirois 2019).

Within management planning, the concept of costs must encompass potential events that could impact the outcomes of actions and evaluate their financial implications. This viewpoint aligns with the understanding that managerial costing systems are integral to organizational frameworks involving diverse subsystems, components, and stakeholders.

## 5.4    Cost Management

The central emphasis of the book lies in manufacturing; however, we acknowledge the essential role of supportive services at various points within the production cycle(s). A typical manufacturing environment consists of primary cost centers (production departments) and secondary cost centers (support departments) contributing to the production process. Consequently, when delving into cost management considerations, it becomes imperative to account for both production and support department dynamics, as depicted in Fig. 5.4.

As previously indicated, the facilitation of production activities is attributed to support departments, thereby necessitating the inclusion of their expenses within production costs. Similar to regular production costs, the costs associated with support departments could include both variable and fixed elements.

### 5.4.1    Main Cost Centers: Production Department

Manufacturing operations occur within production departments, encompassing costs that exhibit variability or constancy. These costs are classified into primary categories within the production department: Direct material, direct labor, indirect costs (such as manufacturing overhead), and secondary support department costs. Direct material and labor costs are directly tied to the production process and are subject to fluctuations. In contrast, manufacturing overhead and potential expenses for support services possess an indirect connection and could display both variability or remain fixed. The allocation of direct costs is relatively straightforward; however, the apportionment of indirect costs presents managerial challenges, particularly in light of increased automation, product diversification, and intricate transactions. These factors contribute to escalated indirect costs and diminished direct labor costs. Badewy et al. (2016) note

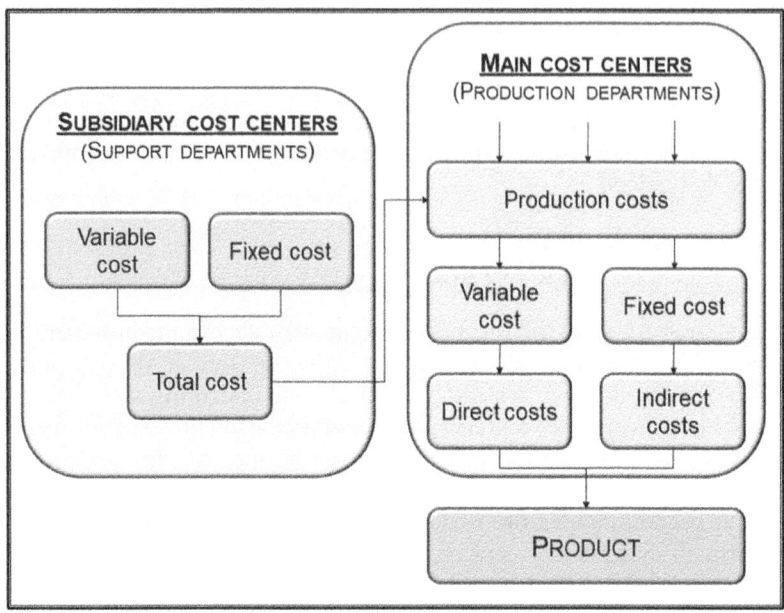

**Fig. 5.4**  Holistic view of manufacturing-related costs

that this challenge is amplified within production departments due to the interplay of both production and non-production indirect costs.

Now, let us examine the significant ramifications concerning managing indirect manufacturing costs. These costs are usually allocated to products utilizing a predetermined rate-per-base-unit, while considering that precise indirect costs become apparent only at the conclusion of the production period. The estimates of indirect costs are, therefore, distributed based on the output of the ongoing production cycle (Foster and Baxendale 2013). Additionally, the volume of production used for cost allocation typically relies on a suitable capacity level estimation (Kuvaieva and Pilova 2021). Information regarding the actual production volume is also solely accessible upon the completion of the production cycle.

In order to control costs efficiently, it is crucial to anticipate and reduce disparities between allocated and factual costs, regardless of initial cost projections or budgets. While the academic distinction between different costing approaches and methods might be prominent, certain approaches and methods could prove more fitting in specific circumstances. Consequently, identifying and contemplating the most appropriate cost driver and production volume is essential.

- Firstly, the concept of a *cost driver* pertains to a variable that directly impacts costs within a defined time frame, as explained by Jiran et al. (2019). Drury (2015) emphasizes the substantial influence of the cost driver on the costs associated with a specific activity. The meticulous choice of this driver is essential to ensure the accurate allocation of costs to various products. The fundamental guideline dictates that cost allocation should be grounded in a driver closely tied to its cause.
- Secondly, the consideration of *production volume* estimates becomes crucial when determining cost allocation rates, encompassing the following volume (or capacity) principles:
  - Theoretical capacity represents the utmost attainable production volume without encountering any breakdowns (Drury 2015).
  - Practical capacity encompasses foreseeable malfunctions and breakdowns, generally ranging from 75% to 85% of the theoretical capacity (Drury 2015).
  - Normal capacity represents the sustained mean projected activity over the long term, excluding unusual fluctuations (Gong et al. 2021).
  - Excess capacity entails the underutilized or unused potential, which could be discerned from overcapacity and idle capacity, as delineated by Gong et al. (2021). Within this context, overcapacity refers to the capability of producing beyond actual requirements, whereas idle capacity conveys a temporary surplus due to a lower demand.

Drawing from the aforementioned context, the choice of capacity levels relies on the intended use of cost particulars. However, Foster and Baxendale (2013) propose that typical capacity is frequently used for the calculation of allocation rates.

### 5.4.2    Secondary Cost Centers: Support Departments

While not playing a direct role in production, support departments provide services to production and other service sectors. As a result, their costs, unrelated to production, could be classified as components of the indirect cost category within the applicable production departments. While a consensus generally exists regarding the allocation of support department costs to the departments utilizing their services, some oppose this practice due to the absence of cost control on the part of the recipient department. Conversely, advocates for such allocation believe that departments benefiting from support services should participate in covering their associated costs.

The selection of an appropriate foundation for allocating support services costs is contingent upon factors such as the level of precision sought, the intended informational objectives, operational complexity, and the nature of the organization. In pursuit of this objective, three overarching approaches are available:

- The direct allocation method involves attributing support department costs to production departments without factoring in interrelationships among support departments (Deevski 2019). The proportionate utilization of provided services determines support cost allocation, and this approach is suitable when excluding cost allocation between support departments results in the least overall production department costs.
- The sequential allocation method involves allocating support department costs to production and other service departments sequentially. This involves selectively allocating support department costs to other support departments in a particular sequence. Notably, once a support department cost has been assigned, it remains unchanged for previously assigned service departments (Deevski 2019). Consequently, the order in which the costs of service departments are allocated is crucial, as it could have implications for the final costs of the end product.
- The reciprocal allocation method is an advancement of the sequential approach. It acknowledges the interdependent service exchange between support departments, with the goal of iteratively distributing support department costs to all other departments until the residual support costs become insignificant (Deevski 2019).

This method stands out as the optimal choice for allocating service department costs, particularly within complex organizational structures. Despite potential perceptions of its complexity and unwieldiness, contemporary computer capabilities streamline intricate calculations, facilitating accurate allocation of support department costs.

## 5.5    Costing

The preceding sections of the chapter explored fundamental theoretical concepts that underpin costing policies and practices. The subsequent sections delve into the practical dimensions of these aspects, focusing on core costing approaches and methods.

### 5.5.1    *Approaches to Costing*

As previously mentioned, a thorough understanding of cost behavior is crucial in cost management, particularly in discerning fixed and variable costs. Given the diverse management objectives and user prerequisites, comprehending this cost-related information becomes paramount. Different management objectives may require distinct costing approaches, leading to dissimilar cost allocations for the end product.

In a broader context, there are two distinct costing approaches (Bunea-Bontaş 2013; Horngren et al. 2015; Drury 2015). Firstly, there is the *direct costing approach*, often referred to as marginal or variable costing due to its emphasis on variable costs. This approach calculates a contribution, which signifies the amount available for recuperating indirect fixed costs. Fixed costs, including depreciation, maintenance, and associated expenses, exhibit relative stability over time and are categorized as periodic costs. This approach itemizes fixed costs separately on the income statement to determine the net profit or loss. Secondly, *absorption costing*, also known as full or total costing, involves allocating variable and fixed costs to the final product, encompassing operational and non-operational costs. This approach segregates the cost of goods sold from selling and administrative costs to calculate gross profit and net profit or loss correspondingly. A comparative analysis of these approaches is presented in Fig. 5.5.

The selection of approaches relies heavily on the intended use of cost information, where internal and external orientations play a pivotal

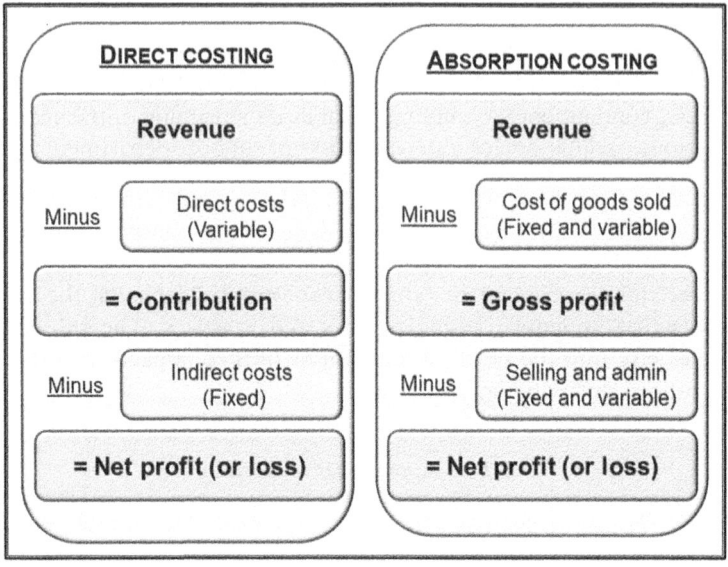

**Fig. 5.5**  Direct costing versus absorption costing

role. Grondskis and Sapkauskiene (2011) recommend employing a direct costing approach to assess *make-or-buy* scenarios, whereas absorption costing is especially fitting for pricing and inventory valuation purposes. Consequently, direct costing is favored for internal decision-making due to its emphasis on contributions to fixed costs and provision of contextually relevant information. External financial reporting necessitates absorption costing, incorporating fixed costs into inventory valuations and profit calculations.

### 5.5.2    *Methods of Costing*

As we delve deeper into the mechanics of cost accounting, we come across various costing methods. These methods fall into two overarching schools of thought: standard costing and operations-centric costing. Each of these methods is shaped by the specific purpose of the cost information, and we will now provide further clarification on these distinctions.

### 5.5.2.1  Standard Costing Systems

The first school of thought follows Generally Accepted Accounting Practices/Principles (GAAP) principles and supports an absorption costing approach (Öztürk 2017). The standard costing approach entails pre-established costs for specific output units and could be traced back to the *First Industrial Revolution* manufacturing sector. While George Norton is acknowledged for his role in advocating standard costing in his 1889 work "Textile Manufacturers' Bookkeeping," G.C. Harrison pioneered one of the earliest comprehensive standard costing systems in the 1910s for the Boss Manufacturing Company in Illinois, United States of America (Chatfield and Vangermeersch 2014).

Avenali et al. (2020) opine that standard costs play a vital role in cost estimation and control, ensuring a balance between practicality and precision. Specifically, the direct assignment of material and labor costs is applied to the product, while the allocation of indirect costs follows a two-stage process involving cost accumulation in overhead pools, followed by allocation based on volume. Standard costing adopts a management-by-exception approach to establish standard costs and manage potential deviations. An essential element of standard costing is variance analysis, which empowers managers to scrutinize disparities between actual and standard costs, thereby facilitating the identification of factors contributing to these variances.

- Direct cost management: Resources directly related to resource consumption comprise the volume of resources utilized and a specific unit price (Rashid 2016). Budgeted or standard costs are initially established through projections of anticipated resource quantities and planned prices per unit, constituting a facet of managerial planning. Two key facets of managerial control must be considered: Firstly, actual outcomes are calculated during operations by multiplying the real resource consumption by the actual unit price paid for resources. Secondly, the standard costs for these actual outputs are derived from the standard input quantity required for the accomplished outputs, multiplied by the standard unit price. The discrepancy between these values constitutes the direct cost variance, which could be dissected further into a variance in quantity (efficiency) and a variance in price (rate). The process of managing these variances is illustrated in Fig. 5.6.

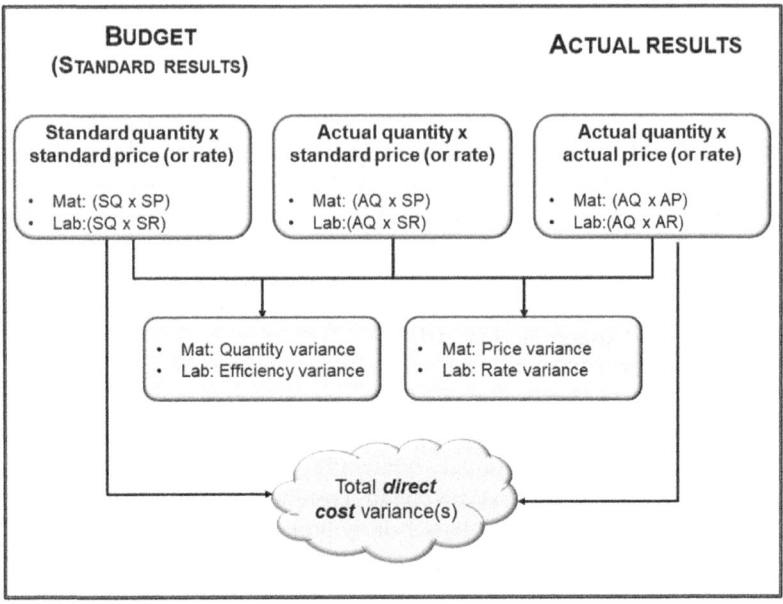

**Fig. 5.6** Management of variances in direct costs

As illustrated in Fig. 5.6, direct material variances could be effectively managed by examining quantity variances (actual quantity used vs. standard quantity) and price variances (actual unit price vs. standard unit price). Similarly, direct labor variances could be managed by analyzing efficiency variances (actual hours used vs. standard hours) and rate variances (actual labor rate vs. standard labor rate).

- Variable indirect cost management: The book's premise posits that indirect costs exhibit a weaker direct correlation with production outputs and encompass both variable and fixed components. Comparable to direct costs, variable indirect costs are subject to control through a flexible-budget variance approach. In contrast to variances in the direct costs, those pertaining to indirect costs tend to be more subjective, accommodating multiple base rates. These rates might include factors such as labor hours, facility area, or other relevant denominators for managerial purposes across diverse indirect cost categories (Foster and Baxendale 2013). This guiding principle maintains uniformity throughout the entire organization. The process of managing variations in indirect costs is illustrated in Fig. 5.7.

Regarding the diagram provided (Fig. 5.7), the variability of indirect cost variables could also be controlled using an *efficiency* variance. This variance assesses the disparity between actual and standard input volumes based on the specific outputs. Additionally, a *spending* variance could be utilized by comparing the actual allocation rates to the standard rates.

- Fixed indirect costs: It has been previously mentioned that fixed indirect costs remain constant regardless of changes in activity levels. As a result, the variations in fixed indirect costs display attributes compared to variable costs. Depending on the chosen costing approach, specific factors require thoughtful consideration. For instance, in a *direct costing* system, products are not burdened with allocated fixed indirect costs; instead, these costs are treated as

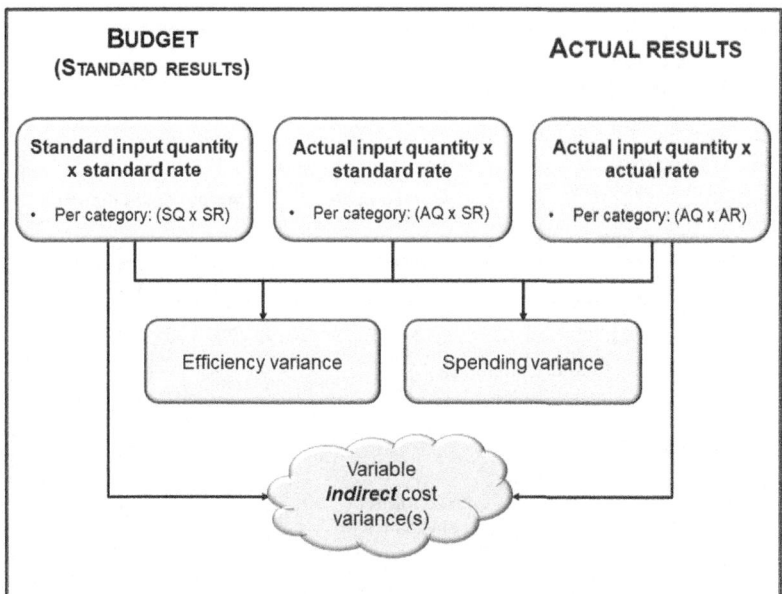

**Fig. 5.7** Management of variances in variable indirect costs

a period cost, offsetting the overall profit (Horngren et al. 2015). Within this system, the variances for fixed indirect costs are determined by contrasting budgeted and actual costs, as exemplified by the following spending variance formula:

$$\text{Spending variance} = \text{Budgeted FC} - \text{Actual FC}.$$

In contrast, an absorption costing system allocates fixed indirect costs to products for inventory assessment and pricing (Foster and Baxendale 2013). This practice could present challenges when dealing with substantial fluctuations in production levels, as fixed costs per unit experience opposite fluctuations compared to production volumes. Similar to how variable cost variances are handled, fixed indirect cost variances within this context are addressed through two distinct viewpoints. Nevertheless, a production volume variance is also taken into account, given that fixed costs are influenced by production volume rather than efficiency, as illustrated in Fig. 5.8.

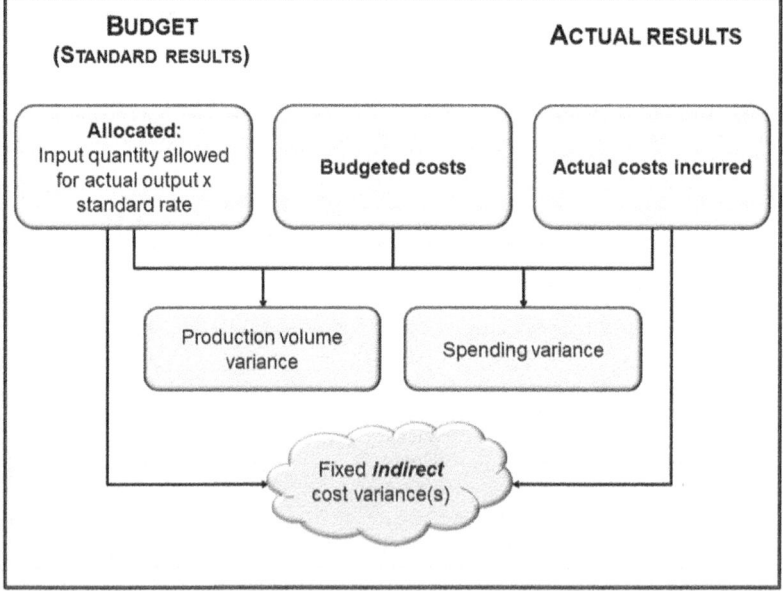

**Fig. 5.8**   Management of variances in fixed indirect costs

In addition to the direct costing approach, the production volume variance represents the variance between the budgeted and allocated fixed indirect costs for the realized actual output in conjunction with the spending variance.

Despite acknowledged dissatisfaction, numerous companies continue to depend on conventional cost calculation methods. This choice is primarily driven by the need to fulfill external financial reporting requirements, such as inventory valuation and cost of goods sold, in accordance with GAAP regulations. Consequently, these managerial cost systems give precedence to financial accounting necessities over internal operational management demands.

### 5.5.2.2 *Operations-Centric Managerial Costing Systems*

The second school of thought aligns costs with organizational operations and the utilization of resources. Novák et al. (2017) reported that the demands stemming from the *Fourth Industrial Revolution* have led to an increase in indirect costs of up to 40%. These approaches seek to establish a correlation between organizational costs and its products. Cost management scholars from the latter part of the twentieth century, including Dominiak and Louderback (1994), Hansen and Mowen (1994), Meigs and Meigs (1995), and Staubus (1988), viewed these approaches as pragmatic managerial tools that allocate indirect costs to the final product based on cost drivers. Contemporary authors like Andersch et al. (2013), Drury (2015), Horngren et al. (2015), Özçelik (2019), and Seal et al. (2012) continue to endorse these approaches, viewing them as supplementary rather than displacing traditional managerial costing systems.

The focus is prioritizing operational activities to obtain accurate cost data, guided by a market-oriented, value-driven management approach, as Grondskis and Sapkauskiene (2011) outlined. This book delves into operational costing methods, including German cost accounting, activity-based costing, and resource consumption accounting. Among these, activity-based costing has been extensively researched due to its compatibility with external financial reporting requirements. However, current research is scarce on the remaining two methods. The subsequent sections provide a chronological overview of the development of these three methods.

- German cost accounting: Referred to as *Grenzplankostenrechnung* (GPK), this method was first developed in the mid-1940s with the aim of optimizing cost accounting data. GPK emphasizes accurate operational modeling to ensure the reliability and uniformity of cost calculation methods. Regarded as a variant of marginal planned cost accounting, GPK facilitates managerial decision-making and enhances the accuracy of product costing (Friedl et al. 2005; Okutmus 2015). Consequently, regarding its conceptual framework, GPK might be classified as a form of direct costing. GPK's approach revolves around capturing the costs of production and service departments that have a causal relationship with the final products. This approach facilitates the assessment of product profitability, starting with the *Contribution Margin: Level I*. This initial level involves deducting variable costs (VC) from revenues. Additionally, within *Contribution Margin: Level II* analysis, GPK might include a standardized per unit rate for fixed costs (FC) that pertain to the products. Costs that cannot be directly assigned to individual products but still have relevance to specific product lines or categories could be allocated in higher levels of profitability reports. The conceptual representation of GPK's methodological principles is presented in Fig. 5.9.

As indicated in Fig. 5.9, *cost-type* accounting involves the identification and analysis of distinct cost classifications along with their corresponding behavioral attributes. Conversely, *cost-center* accounting plays a crucial role within the context of GPK, concentrating on areas of functional accountability. Two distinct varieties of cost centers exist: Primary, which directly contribute to the ultimate product; and secondary, which furnish support services to primary cost centers. Additionally, the concept of *product costing* entails aggregating costs linked to products. *Profitability management* further integrates these aforementioned elements by deducting product costs from product revenues while considering diverse levels and varieties of fixed and support service costs.

GPK places a significant emphasis on conducting multilevel contribution margin analyses, thereby facilitating the effective profitability management for operational and strategic decision-making purposes. The core principles underpinning GPK are centered

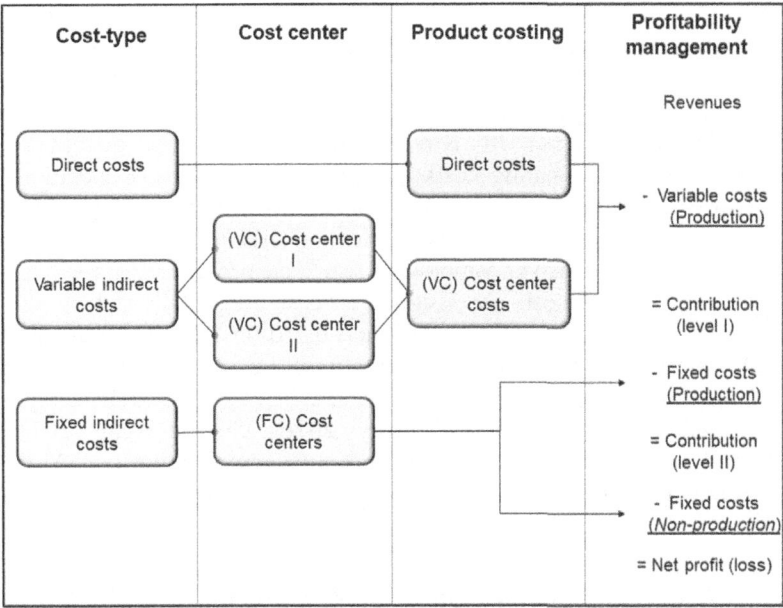

**Fig. 5.9** Conceptual presentation of GPK's principles

around operational processes, identification of cost drivers, and a comprehensive understanding of the organizational implications; therefore establishing it as a highly valuable instrument for cost management. Although its historical usage has been prevalent in organizations characterized by complex operational processes, the applicability of GPK extends successfully to even simpler manufacturing processes. Just as with other complex and integrated managerial costing systems, the implementation of GPK requires a sophisticated Enterprise Resource Planning (ERP) system to serve as its technological backbone.

- Activity-based costing: Following GPK's development by about three decades, the inception of activity-based costing (ABC) in the early 1970s comes to light. Okutmus (2015) believes that the emergence of ABC stemmed from the inadequacy of traditional (volume-based) costing methods to furnish sufficient cost management information in the contemporary business environment.

ABC is categorized as an absorption costing approach due to its practice of attributing fixed costs (FC) and variable costs (VC) to the costs associated with products. Its primary objective, alongside direct costs, involves estimating the total cost linked to an organization's range of products. ABC is renowned as a precise and quantitative method for estimating costs. It systematically analyzes operational activities, distinguishing between value-adding and nonvalue-adding actions, and emphasizes waste reduction over mere cost allocation. The ABC approach encompasses a two-stage procedure. In the initial phase, indirect costs are assigned to cost pools, followed by allocating these pooled costs to products based on activity requirements in the second stage. The two-stage procedure outlined above finds concurrence in contemporary sources, like Alami and ElMaraghy (2020), Dwivedi and Chakraborty (2016), Go and Weng (2021), and Jiran et al. (2019). The conceptual representation of ABC's methodological principles is depicted in Fig. 5.10.

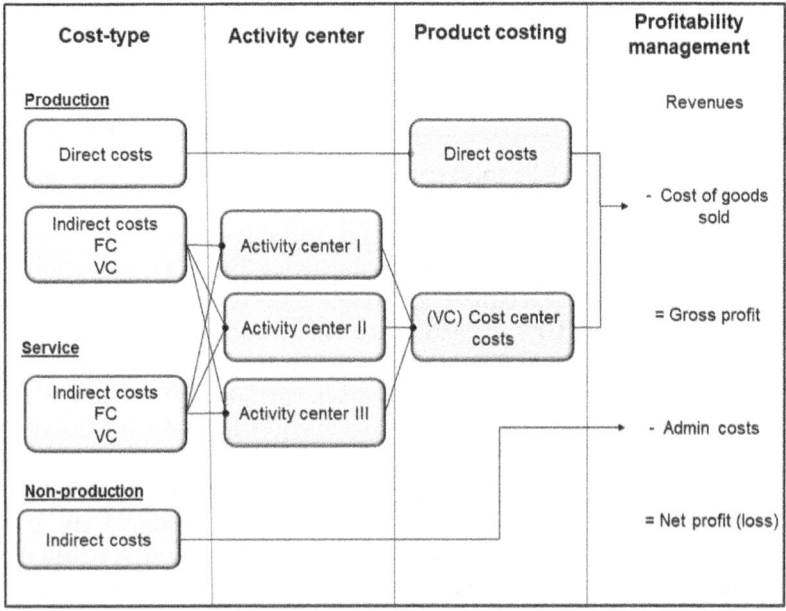

**Fig. 5.10** Conceptual presentation of ABC's principles

As depicted, *cost-type* accounting involves identifying and classifying distinct direct and indirect cost categories, followed by examining their behavioral traits prior to their allocation to activity centers. In parallel, *activity-center* accounting encompasses allocating indirect costs to activity centers, focusing on analyzing cost behavior and the value-added efficacy of diverse activities. Furthermore, *product costing* involves the inclusion of two supplementary steps: The determination of cost driver rates for each activity based on their causal connection to cost incurrence and the allocation of product costs based on the level of activity consumption. The amalgamation of these facets is achieved in *profitability management*, wherein product costing information is subtracted from product revenues, subsequently acknowledging varying degrees of fixed and support services costs.

However, ABC is built upon a foundation of two key assumptions: First, the presence of homogeneous cost drivers, wherein standardized cost drivers propel costs within each individual cost center; and second, the utilization of proportional cost drivers, which causes cost centers to experience proportionate variations in costs whenever there is a change in activity levels. The underlying assumptions of ABC could lead to complex and highly detailed operational examinations, frequently resulting in overly complicated managerial costing systems. This complexity has contributed to the discontinuation of many ABC systems and drawbacks in furnishing internal decision-making support. Often, ABC systems are rejected due to their perceived complexity or untimeliness in guiding operational decisions. A possible alternative, known as *time-driven ABC*, offers an alternative approach to address these complexities. It simplifies the aspect of operational analysis in the design of cost systems by making time the primary cost driver for costs (Alami and ElMaraghy 2020; Özçelik 2019). However, some argue that this approach undermines ABC's fundamental purpose and benefits, which is to pinpoint the activity drivers responsible for incurring costs.

- Resource consumption accounting: As an evolutionary approach in the realm of GPK and ABC, resource consumption accounting (RCA) aims to integrate the strengths of GPK's emphasis on resources and ABC's focus on operational activities (Okutmus 2015; Perkins and Stovall 2011). Formulating an RCA managerial costing system involves delineating connections between production and support departments, product costs, and shared fixed costs. In this context, primary costs stem from resource centers, whereas secondary costs are allocated from other resource centers; overall resource costs could be either fixed or proportional, depending upon the relationship between input and output quantities. Figure 5.11 illustrates the conceptual cost flow within an RCA process.

As illustrated, *resource-type* accounting involves the identification and examination of various proportional and fixed cost classifications based on their behavioral characteristics. *Resource pool* accounting focuses on aggregating costs related to homogeneous resources within a specific scope of responsibility, similar to cost center accounting in GPK. Additionally, *production activity center* accounting establishes the connections between resources and the products that utilize those resources. Furthermore, in *product costing*, costs are apportioned to products as activities consume resources, considering the differentiation between proportional and

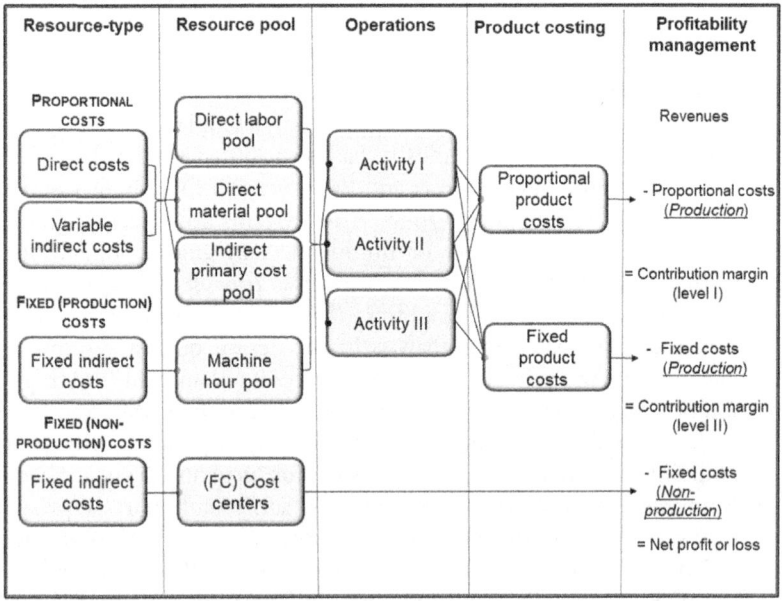

**Fig. 5.11** Conceptual presentation of RCA's principles

fixed costs. Enhancing *profitability management* involves integrating the above-mentioned components, achieved through subtracting both proportional and fixed cost information from revenue figures.

While RCA could be considered a hybrid system, its core nature aligns with a direct (variable) costing approach. It distinguishes between fixed and variable costs while integrating resources and marginal costs, similar to the emphasis seen in GPK. Consequently, RCA might not be suitable for external financial reporting, given its deviation from the principles of full costing and non-causal cost allocation required by GAAP.

### 5.5.2.3   *Related Concepts*

The aforementioned cost methodologies aim to pinpoint accurate and relevant costs while evaluating indirect costs to ensure precise calculations of profits. However, they frequently overlook the significant operational aspect of resource constraints. Apart from these methodologies, there are other cost management concepts centered around operations that are worth mentioning:

- Theory of constraints: Although it is not primarily focused on costing methodology, this concept serves as an important methodology that emphasizes the significance of understanding operations within cost management. It aims to identify and remove constraints, improve resource utilization, optimize production processes' efficiency, and tackle bottlenecks (Kadhim et al. 2020). As a result, its fundamental procedure involves systematically identifying and resolving constraints, thereby fostering improved production throughput and increasing profitability.
- Throughput accounting: This production planning methodology developed from the theory of constraints (Kadhim et al. 2020), aims to maximize profit in scenarios where constraints exist within the production processes of multiple products. The approach utilizes marginal costing principles to determine the most suitable product within a given context. Kadhim et al. (2020) emphasize that the central focus is achieving overall organizational profitability rather than solely analyzing individual product-level profit margins.
- Lean accounting: This operational philosophy focuses on eliminating inefficiencies and improving processes. It incorporates cost-reduction

strategies (Arora and Soral 2017), which involve the utilization of value stream and engineering analysis techniques for cost reduction (Al-Qady and El-Helbawy 2016). In order to support decision-making, accounting practices should adapt and align with lean principles (Man and Răvas 2017). The framework of lean accounting involves allocating costs based on relevant value streams, monitoring revenue and variable costs, and utilizing simplified inventory valuation methods. Additionally, it incorporates non-financial measures to assess operational performance, streamlines cost-collection processes, and aims to reduce the number of cost centers.

- Target costing: This refers to a strategic planning approach that considers factors such as product pricing, costs, and profit margins (Al-Qady and El-Helbawy 2016). It focuses on developing products in response to market demand and the willingness of consumers to pay (Zengin and Ada 2010). In cases where a product cannot be manufactured within the intended cost parameters, the design project might be terminated. Target costing is employed for continual monitoring that spans the design phase through the entire product life cycle, helping develop profitable products from the outset. This approach contrasts with the conventional method of creating a product solely from an engineering perspective and later grappling with cost-related challenges.

## 5.6   In Conclusion

The chapter's objective is to offer a comprehensive view of the cost accounting component within managerial costing systems that an organization can adopt. It began with exploring the operational environment, from job to process costing. Particular attention is given to understanding cost behavior and its ramifications for management. Moreover, the discourse delves into the correlation between primary cost centers and support cost centers. The chapter further covers (i) approaches to costing centered around variable and fixed costs, along with their associated objectives; (ii) various costing methodologies, including German cost accounting, activity-based costing, and resource consumption accounting; and (iii) a succinct overview of the theory of constraints, throughput accounting, lean accounting, and target costing.

The upcoming chapter will delve into the first eADR iteration in the managerial costing system process model design, namely the problem refinement aspect thereof.

## References

Alami, D. and ElMaraghy, W. 2020. Traditional and activity based aggregate job costing model. *53rd CIRP Conference on Manufacturing Systems 2020*, Chicago, IL.

Al-Qady, M. and El-Helbawy, S. 2016. Integrating target costing and resource consumption accounting. *Journal of Applied Management Accounting Research*, 14(1):39–54.

Andersch, A., Buehlmann, U., Palmer, J., Wiedenbeck, J.K. and Lawser, S. 2013. Product costing program for wood component manufacturers. *Forest Products Journal*, 63(7/8):247–256.

Arora, V. and Soral, G. 2017. Conceptual issues in a lean accounting: A review. *Journal of Accounting Research and Audit Practices*, 16(3):54–63.

Avenali, A., Boitani, A., Catalano, G., Matteucci, G. and Monticini, A. 2020. Standard costs of regional public rail passenger transport: Evidence from Italy. *Applied Economics*, 52(15):1704–1717. https://doi.org/10.1080/000 36846.2019.1677852.

Badewy, M., Ghany, M. and Kandel, Y. 2016. Time Driven ABC as a new approach for allocating costs in the Egyptian manufacturing companies—Case study. *Journal of Alternative Perspectives in the Social Sciences*, 8(2):248–262.

Banker, R.D., Byzalov, D., Fang, S. and Liang, Y. 2018. Cost management research. *Journal of Management Accounting Research*, 30(3):187–209.

Bozkurt, O., Dokur, Ş. and Yildirim, A. 2014. The importance of cost calculation method in the accounting and management of Turkish operating costs: a research within the scope of TAS-2. *International Journal of Academic Research in Accounting, Finance and Management Sciences*, 4(2):38–46.

Bradbury, M.E. and Scott, T. 2018. Do managers forecast asymmetric cost behaviour? *Australian Journal of Management*, 43(4):538–554.

Bunea-Bontaş, C.A. 2013. The cost of production under direct costing and absorption costing—A comparative approach. *Analele Universităţii Constantin Brâncuşi din Târgu Jiu: Seria Economie*, 2(2):123–129.

Chatfield, M. and Vangermeersch, R. 2014. *Control: Classic model in History of accounting: An international encyclopaedia.* pp. 174–175.

Cooper, A.A. and Stoner, J.C. 2021. The price of hiring resident assistants: An analysis of human capital, opportunity costs, and personnel wages. *The Journal of College and University Student Housing*, 47(3):76–91.

Da Silva, A., Zonatto, V.C., Magro, C.B.D. and Klann, R. 2019. Sticky costs behavior and earnings management. *Brazilian Business Review*, 16(2):191–206. https://doi.org/10.15728/bbr.2019.16.2.6.

Deevski, S. 2019. Management of indirect costs—Mathematical methods for cost allocation. *Trakia Journal of Sciences*, 17(1):496–503. https://doi.org/10.15547/tjs.2019.s.01.080.

Dominiak, G.F. and Louderback, J.G. 1994. *Managerial accounting*. Cincinnati, OH: South Western.

Drury, C. 2015. *Management and cost accounting*. 9th ed. Melbourne: Cengage Learning, Australia.

Dwivedi, R. and Chakraborty, S. 2016. Adoption of an activity based costing model in an Indian steel plant. *Business: Theory and Practice*, 17(4):289–298. https://doi.org/10.3846/btp.17.10864.

Foster, B.P. and Baxendale, S.J. 2013. Accounting for the Cost of Unused Capacity in an Economic Downturn: Companies' Responses to SFAS 151. *The CPA Journal*, May:20–26.

Friedl, G., Kupper, H.U. and Pedell, B. 2005. Relevance added: Combining ABC with German cost accounting. *Strategic Finance*, June:56–61.

Go, J.A. and Weng, C.Y. 2021. Process mapping and activity-based costing of the intravitreal injection procedure. *Current Eye Research*, 46(5):694–703. https://doi.org/10.1080/02713683.2020.1825747.

Gong, D.C., Chen, P.S. and Wang, S.J. 2021. Simulation study of impact of capacity reservation threshold on order fulfilment. *International Journal of Simulation Modelling*, 20(1):17–28.

Grondskis, G. and Sapkauskiene, A. 2011. Cost accounting information for product mix design. *Economics and Management*, 16:48–53.

Hansen, D.R. and Mowen, M.M. 1994. *Management accounting*. Cincinnati, OH: South-Western.

Horngren, C.T., Datar, S.M. and Rajan, M.V. 2015. *Cost accounting: A managerial emphasis*. 15th ed. Boston, MA: Pearson.

Hosomi, S. and Nagasawa, S. 2018. Empirical study on asymmetric cost behaviour: Analysis of the sticky costs of local public enterprises. *Asia-Pacific Management Accounting Journal*, 13(2):55–82.

Hultman, J.A. 2021. Know your relevant costs before making financial decisions: Small improvements in your decision-making process will add up over time. *Podiatry Management*, February:134–138.

Jiran, N.S., Gholami, H., Mahmood, S., Saman, M.Z.M., Yusof, N.M., Draskovic, V. and Javovic, R. 2019. Application of activity-based costing in estimating the costs of manufacturing process. *Transformations in Business & Economics*, 18(2B (47B):839–860.

Kadhim, H.K., Najm, K.J. and Kadhim, H.N. 2020. Using throughput accounting for cost management and performance assessment: Constraint theory approach. *TEM Journal*, 9(2):763–769.

Kuvaieva, T.V. and Pilova, K.P. 2021. Forms of organization of production activity of enterprises in terms of probabilistic nature of demand. *Scientific Bulletin of National Mining University*, 4:177–184. https://doi.org/ 10.33271/nvngu/2021-4/177.

Krumwiede, K.R. and Walden, W.D. 2013. Dream chocolate company: Choosing a costing system. *Issues in Accounting Education*, 28(3):637–652. https:// doi.org/10.2308/iace-50464.

Labro, E. 2019. Costing systems. *Foundations and Trends in Accounting*, 13(3–4):267–404. https://doi.org/10.1561/1400000058.

Lewis, J. (n.d.). Operational costing vs. process costing systems. https:// smallbusiness.chron.com/gaapapproved-costing-methods-80589.html. Date accessed: December 26, 2021.

Li, W., Natarajan, R., Zhao, Y. and Zheng, K. 2021. The effect of management control mechanisms through risk-taking incentives on asymmetric cost behaviour. *Review of Quantitative Finance and Accounting*, 56:219–243. https://doi.org/10.1007/s11156-020-00891-z.

Magheed, B.A. 2016. The determines of the sticky cost behavior in the Jordanian industrial companies listed in Amman stock market. *Journal of Accounting, Business and Management*, 23(1):64–81.

Man, M. and Răvas, B. 2017. Integrating the exigencies of lean manufacturing in the accounting system of lean thinking organisations. *Annals of the University of Petroşani, Economics*, 17(1):139–154.

Meigs, R.F. and Meigs, W.B. 1995. *Accounting: the basis for business decisions*. New York: McGraw-Hill.

Novák, P., Dvorský, J., Popesko, B. and Strouhal, J. 2017. Analysis of overhead cost behavior: case study on decision-making approach. *Journal of International Studies*, 10(1):74–91. https://doi.org/10.14254/2071-8330.2017/ 10-1/5.

Okutmus, E. 2015. Resource consumption accounting with cost dimension and an application in a glass factory. *International Journal of Academic Research in Accounting, Finance and Management Sciences*, 5(1):46–57.

Özçelik, F. 2019. Kapasite Maliyet Yönetimi Açısından Maliyetleme Yöntemlerinin Karşılaştırılması (Comparing costing methods in terms of capacity cost management). *Business and Management Studies: An International Journal*, 7(4):1311–1333. https://doi.org/10.15295/bmij.v7i4.1171.

Öztürk, C. 2017. The role and current status of IFRS in the completion of national accounting rules—Evidence from Turkey. *Accounting in Europe*, 14(1–2):226–234. https://doi.org/10.1080/17449480.2017.1304647.

Perkins, D. and Stovall, O. 2011. Resource consumption accounting: Where does it fit? *Journal of Applied Business Research*, 27(5):41–52. https://doi.org/10.19030/jabr.v27i5.5591.

Raef, R., Cokins, G., Hicks, D., Krumwiede, K., Swain, M. and White, L. 2019a. *Developing an effective managerial cost model.* Statements on Management Accounting. Institute of Management Accountants (IMA), Montvale, N.J.

Raef, R., Cokins, G., Hicks, D., Krumwiede, K., Swain, M. and White, L. 2019b. *Costing system attributes that support good decision making.* Statements on Management Accounting. Institute of Management Accountants (IMA), Montvale, N.J.

Rashid, M. 2016. Standard costing practices in listed pharmaceutical industries in Bangladesh. *The Cost and Management*, 44(6):44–50.

Reynoso, L.F.L., Vela-Beltrán-del-Río, C. and Martínez-Berrones, J.L. 2021. Sticky costs and expenses are not alike: Mexican reality. *Journal of Accounting, Business and Management*, 28(1):14–30.

Seal, W., Garrison, R.H. and Noreen, E.W. 2012. *Management accounting.* 4th ed. New York: McGraw-Hill.

Sicuro Corrêa, L.M., Augusto, M.R.A. and Marcilese, M. 2018. Competing analyses and differential cost in the production of non-subject relative clauses. *Glossa: A Journal of General Linguistics*, 3(1):62. 1–22. https://doi.org/10.5334/gjgl.401.

Sirois, L.P. 2019. The psychology of sunk cost: A classroom experiment. *The Journal of Economic Education*, 50(4):398–409. https://doi.org/10.1080/00220485.2019.1654954.

Staubus, G.J. 1988. *Activity costing for decisions.* New York: Garland Publishing.

Togha, M., Nadjafi-Semnani, F., Martami, F., Mohammadshirazi, Z., Vahidpour, N., Akbari-sari, A. and Daroudi, R. 2021. Economic burden of medication-overuse headache in Iran: direct and indirect costs. *Neurological Sciences*, 42:1869–1877. https://doi.org/10.1007/s10072-020-04716-8.

Yegínboy, E.Y. and Y"uksel, I. 2015. Hospital administration in the cardiology clinic: Job order costing method outpatient diagnosis of calculation of cost. *Dokuz Eylul University Journal of Graduate School of Social Sciences*, 17(3):409–443. https://doi.org/10.16953/deusbed.91942.

Zengin, Y. and Ada, E. 2010. Cost management through product design: Target costing approach. *International Journal of Production Research*, 48(19):5593–5611.

Zhang, J. and Liu, Y. 2020. Study on estimation method of port container handling cost based on interval analysis. *Journal of Coastal Research*, 95:979–984.

# CHAPTER 6

# First eADR Iteration: Problem Refinement

The preceding chapters established the literary groundwork for designing effective managerial costing systems. The current chapter builds upon the literature review and addresses the initial sub-objective. Within the framework of the book's objective, this chapter specifically examines the complexities of the three identified pillars. As this iteration is part of Phase I (see Table 2.2), the research team consists of industry experts with experience in manufacturing management and related consulting. The problem is further clarified by outlining the guiding principles for this iteration, followed by a methodical examination of the process and outcomes based on the ADR stages.

## 6.1 Guiding Principles for the Iteration of Diagnosis

The diagnosis iteration is the starting point for investigating the relationships between cost accounting and business processes within a systems thinking framework. The following context provides an illustration of this (Fig. 6.1).

Mullarkey and Hevner (2018) suggest that the problem-centric eADR diagnosis phase offers contextual understanding within the research domain. Hence, as detailed later, the applied research approach in

P. W. Buys, *Crafting Efficiency in Managerial Costing System Design*, https://doi.org/10.1007/978-981-97-0934-2_6

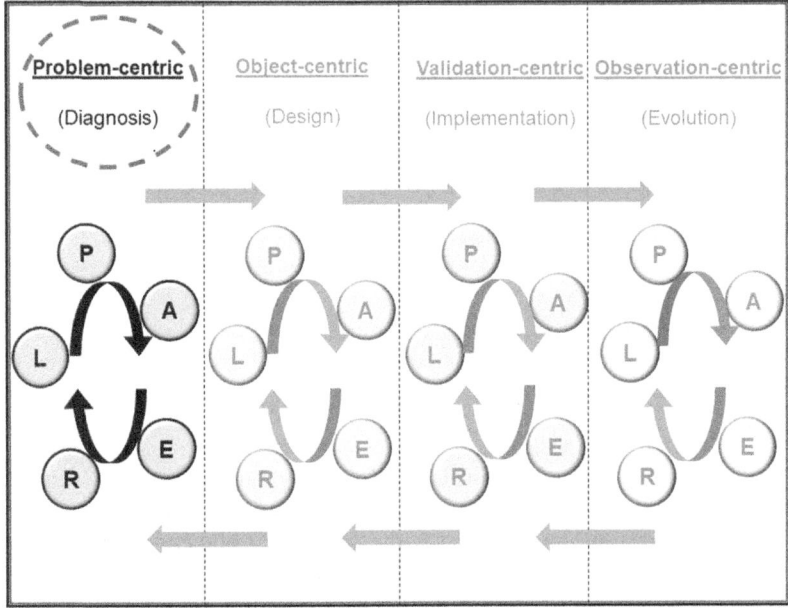

**Fig. 6.1**  Problem-centric eADR diagnosis iteration

this eADR iteration is founded on the four ADR stages (presented in Table 6.1) and their corresponding seven guiding principles.

Table 6.1 provides a concise overview of the ADR stages and their relevance within the context of this chapter. To contextualize the problem, it entails the integration of problem-solving and design-thinking methodologies, as well as continual collaboration with practitioners. By employing this approach, the diagnostic iteration aids in identifying challenges and generating significant contextual knowledge. The subsequent sections of the chapter then proceed to execute these stages in a sequential manner.

**Table 6.1**  Diagnosis activities

| ADR stages and principles | | Key activities |
|---|---|---|
| **Stage 1**: Problem formulation | **Principle 1**: Practice-inspired<br>**Principle 2**: Theory-ingrained | • Emphasize the actual significance of modern manufacturing and cost management<br>• Highlight earlier research findings regarding the importance of effective cost management<br>• Consider the relationships among the pillars<br>• Validate the problem context by consulting relevant industry experts |
| **Stage 2**: Building, intervention, and evaluation | **Principle 3**: Reciprocal shaping<br>**Principle 4**: Mutually influential roles<br>**Principle 5**: Authentic and concurrent evaluation | Based on the three pillars, the following were highlighted:<br>• Develop process flow models as developmental artifacts<br>• Review, assess, and refine these process flows within the defined research problem context through interactions with industry experts<br>The stage was completed during collaborative researcher–practitioner interactions |

(continued)

**Table 6.1** (continued)

| ADR stages and principles | | Key activities |
|---|---|---|
| **Stage 3**: Reflection and learning | **Principle 6**: Guided emergence | The knowledge acquired formed the foundation for contextual reflection and learning |
| **Stage 4**: Formalization of learning | **Principle 7**: Generalized outcomes | The knowledge gained from the aforementioned stages was used as the foundation to create developmental guides for each pillar, which can serve as systematic road maps for data collection |

## 6.2   Problem Formulation

### 6.2.1   Framing the Problem

Practice-orientated research seeks to produce knowledge that is applicable to particular types of problems. Sein et al. (2011) propose that problem formulation and conceptualization are essential in the process of formulating and diagnosing problems that were *experienced*, emphasizing the integration of practical insights into theoretical frameworks. In a similar vein, Rogerson and Scott (2014) argue that a solution's *theoretical underpinnings* play a crucial role in gaining acceptance. The motivation behind the creation of this book stemmed from the recognition that truly effective managerial costing systems were infrequently found.

In Chapter 1, the research justification and background explore historical and contemporary viewpoints on the manufacturing environment—highlighting its continued importance as a significant driver in global economies. The emergence of dynamic and agile technologies during the *Fourth Industrial Revolution* was acknowledged for its potential impact on manufacturing. Additionally, the importance of comprehensively understanding organizational costs and effectively managing them was recognized as essential for ensuring the creation of economic value. Moreover, the examination of pertinent academic literature, such as Appelbaum et al. (2017) and Labro (2019), revealed that despite the expectation for management accounting, including cost management to prioritize future-oriented perspectives, it primarily relies on the external reporting of past data. Consequently, numerous managerial costing systems that emphasize internal perspectives are considered to be conceptually misaligned and misguided.

Scholars have put forth the viewpoint that adopting cost management strategies based on organizational activities enhances the efficacy of managerial decision-making (Bhaskar 2018; James 2013). Chapters 3–5 serve the purpose of offering theoretical support for the subsequent discussions. These chapters present three fundamental pillars namely, systems thinking, business processes, and cost accounting. These pillars were identified as the basis for constructing the model with the goal of illustrating the inherent complexity involved in establishing efficient managerial costing systems. During the process of refining the problem class, it became apparent that the core of a managerial costing system lies in its capacity to furnish relevant data regarding costs and resource utilization. This information plays a vital role in assisting managerial objectives within a dynamic business environment.

### 6.2.2    Research Problem Corroboration

Despite offering theoretical contextualization of the problem, it was considered essential to validate this understanding by incorporating practical experiences from the industry. Industry experts were posed guided questions derived from the insights gained through the literature review. Although the industry experts were given certain background information, the explicit emphasis on the specific details of the three pillars (topic concepts) was intentionally minimized to avoid confirmation bias and promote unbiased expert opinions. The questions and their corresponding summative responses are presented below:

- *Question*: What is your opinion on cost management's role, function, and importance in organizational value creation and economic viability?

  *Answer*: Firstly, it is essential to prioritize cost-effective decision-making and the maximization of profitability when implementing consistent cost principles in various jurisdictions. This objective is accomplished by allocating sales and determining the jurisdiction or plant responsible for meeting production demand. Secondly, in the contemporary business environment, stakeholder management is gaining growing significance with cost management playing a crucial role in devising, executing, and monitoring advantageous business strategies that meet the demands of stakeholders. Thirdly, with regard to its *functionality*, cost management encompasses a perpetual procedure that includes four key stages: Resource planning; activity evaluation; budgeting; and control. This approach facilitates proficient financial oversight and offers operational insights aimed at improving the efficiency of business processes. Finally, in relation to the triple bottom line and its *significance*, decision-making is not exclusively centered around profit maximization but takes into account the social, environmental, and economic consequences. As a result, effective cost management assumes critical importance in evaluating the present business performance across various aspects, offering essential insights for decision-making, and securing the long-term sustainability of resources for achieving success.

- *Question*: What is your opinion on the effectiveness of managerial costing systems in achieving their objectives (per the above response)?

*Answer*: It is essential for an organization's profitability to identify and address cost issues effectively. Presently, cost management is primarily employed for operational and reporting objectives rather than strategically contributing value to the organization's activities. Considering the constantly changing business landscape, it is crucial to evaluate and modify the parameter settings of a managerial costing system regularly. A successful managerial costing system should demonstrate adaptability and agility, encompassing variables beyond the microeconomic environment. At present, managerial costing systems heavily rely on human intervention and may evolve to integrate artificial intelligence (AI). This transition has the potential to enhance the system's agility, resilience, and value creation capabilities.

- *Question*: What would you consider to be sound business or management principles able to ensure relevant and supportive management information is generated?

*Answer*: Create an independent cost department that implements cost techniques effectively to meet CAPEX objectives consistently. Guarantee precise and comprehensible definitions and communication of goals and deliverables. Take into account both the micro and macroeconomic contexts, and analyze and understand the actual costs throughout the organization's value chain and system. Conduct periodic evaluations and updates of systems to ensure their continued relevance and adaptability to changes in the micro or macro business environment.

- *Question*: What is your opinion on systems thinking as a foundational design approach to contribute to more effective managerial costing system design?

*Answer*: A comprehensive understanding of a managerial costing system should extend beyond the organization's accountants and include the production departments. When the managerial costing system is aligned with the production systems, it becomes widely accepted and advantageous for the entire organization. By adopting a systems thinking approach, one could enhance the accuracy of forecasting by considering the interconnectedness and impact of variables within the surrounding structure. Systems thinking offers a more disciplined approach, taking into account specified relationships, models, and the business environment—in contrast to the cause-and-effect thinking of a linear approach. Embracing a systems thinking approach enables a holistic assessment, facilitating a change in perspective to navigate effectively the complexities of dynamic social systems within the workplace, the overall business, and even the broader economy.

- *Question*: Would a managerial costing system cognizant of business processes contribute to more effective cost management?

  *Answer*: Distinct challenges arise in different jurisdictions at various times, which creates opportunities for strategic decision-making. For instance, shifting production to regions with lower costs during specific seasons may be advantageous, such as moving production to Europe in winter rather than South Africa. Embracing a systems thinking approach to cost management allows for a comprehensive understanding of an organization's interconnected components, temporal progression, and interrelationships. This perspective facilitates the achievement of business objectives and the alignment of operational activities, reporting, and strategies with internal and external variables in the business environment. The systems thinking approach acknowledges the cause-and-effect relationships and their impact on business activities and decisions, ultimately contributing to the attainment of predetermined goals. By perceiving the organization as a dynamic entity that both influenced and is influenced by all stakeholders within its markets and operations, management could make more informed decisions and foster a holistic perspective.

- *Question*: Given the above, what is your opinion on a three-pillar approach, taking cognizance of systems thinking, business process, and cost accounting aspects, as a departure point in understanding effective cost management?

  *Answer*: Applying a systems thinking methodology to cost management fosters a comprehensive understanding and accountability of managerial costing systems across company functions. This approach facilitates the establishment of consistent and dependable managerial costing systems, empowering informed decision-making in the short and long term. Embracing a systems thinking approach enables managerial costing systems to transcend linear reporting—empowering managers to improve business activities continuously based on accurate and timely information. Moreover, this approach facilitates swift responses and anticipates changes in the operational landscape. The benefits of enhanced efficiencies and business agility arise from viewing business activities within the broader context of the systems thinking approach. Rather than solely concentrating on detailed aspects, this approach takes into account the impact of various factors in the larger business environment. Consequently, conventional problems that may have been perceived as threats or weaknesses under linear thinking could be reclassified as opportunities when approached through a systems thinking lens, considering their broader impact on the business environment.

According to the aforementioned responses, our research problem and approach have been validated. The significance of stakeholders has been acknowledged by experts, who emphasized the role of cost management in enhancing organizational performance. The experts further highlighted the importance of acknowledging social and environmental obligations. Additionally, they pointed out that existing managerial costing systems mainly concentrate on reporting rather than improving organizational performance. They remarked that these systems are frequently rigid, obsolete, and heavily reliant on human intervention, proposing that the utilization of AI could enhance their capacity to facilitate value creation. The experts in the field maintain that adopting systems thinking could enable a comprehensive understanding of organizational structures and offer a structured methodology for designing managerial costing systems. This approach advocates a contextual viewpoint that aligns with the changing demands of contemporary times, departing from traditional linear thinking. Building upon the previous discussion, it was stressed by the experts that the application of systems thinking plays a crucial role in facilitating the examination of business processes within an organization. Such analysis holds significant importance for effective cost management practices and desired outcomes, thereby establishing itself as an indispensable component of system design. Furthermore, systems thinking empowers stakeholders to perceive the organization as a dynamic entity akin to a living organism. The experts acknowledged the value of employing a three-pillar approach, which promotes an integrated design of managerial costing systems, in contrast to conventional linear thinking.

## 6.3    Building, Intervention, and Evaluation

During each iteration of the eADR process, the artifact underwent design and assessment activities specific to that iteration. These activities encompassed the early analysis of concepts, requirements, and design principles. This stage in the overall process incorporated the principles of reciprocal shaping, mutually influential roles, and authentic evaluation, which actively engaged legitimate stakeholders in shaping the solution.

The diagnostic artifacts established a fundamental understanding to steer the subsequent process modeling activities. A set of three conceptual process flow models was formulated by the researcher–practitioner team, with each model specifically targeting one of the primary pillars. The objective of these models was to emphasize the intricate and interconnected nature of the undertaking—paving the way for the creation of the model. The researcher completed the initial information for these process flow models, which were subsequently shared with industry experts to obtain their input and suggestions. The agreed-upon flows are presented.

### 6.3.1    Systems Thinking Process Flow Model

Figure 6.2 showcases the process flow model of systems thinking, which is derived from theoretical foundations presented in Chapter 3, along with valuable input from industry experts.

The process flow of systems thinking demonstrates the design process through three clearly defined levels, as outlined below:

- Firstly, the objective of incorporating systems theory considerations is threefold: (i) to provide clarity regarding the categorization of the managerial costing system, aiding the system designer(s) in understanding its artificial, conceptual, and open-system characteristics; (ii) to establish an initial understanding of the system's environment, encompassing its operational context, input and output specifications, as well as the elements and relationships within the (sub-) systems; and (iii) to enhance the design framework by assessing the

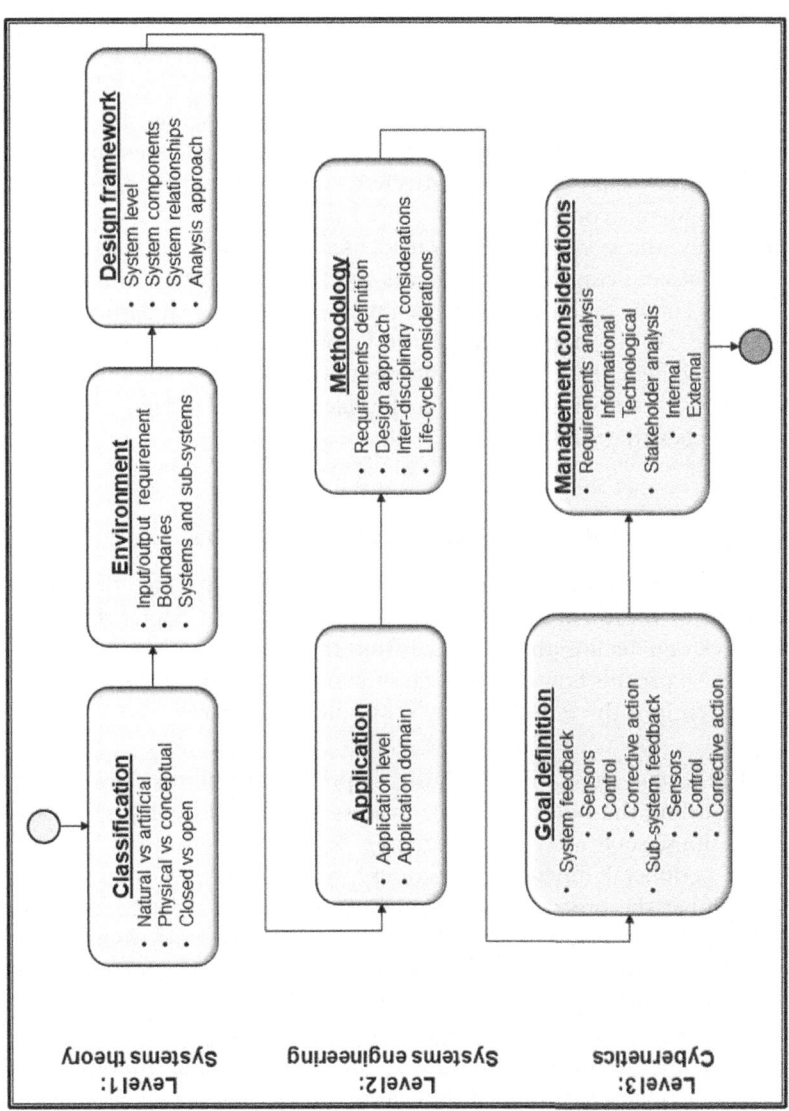

Fig. 6.2   Process flow of system thinking analysis

system at a holistic level, identifying the essential building blocks, and contextualizing the analysis methodology.

- Secondly, the section on systems engineering section places emphasizes on the identification and definition of the system's application level(s) and domain(s). This process includes taking into account additional methodological factors, such as determining the system's requirements, understanding its functional context, identifying the organizational departments affected, and foreseeing the life cycle of the system's components.
- Finally, the cybernetics section focuses on supporting system goals and placing emphasis on feedback mechanisms to attain those goals. This entails determining the required inputs and establishing techniques to monitor, manage, and control progress. Additionally, identifying and defining the informational and technological requirements, along with considering the relevant stakeholders, are crucial aspects within this context.

### 6.3.2    Business Processes Process Flow

The process flow of business processes, presented in Fig. 6.3, is an extension of the theoretical foundations discussed in Chapter 4. It also integrates valuable insights obtained from the industry experts.

The final process flow demonstrates the structure of business processes, categorized into three discrete levels, as outlined below:

- The initial section of the business process definition offers clarity regarding the objective of the process model. This includes considerations, such as (i) differentiating between core, critical support, or peripheral functions at various process levels; (ii) determining whether the process is managerial or operational through classification levels; (iii) examining life-cycle-related aspects discussed earlier; and (iv) assessing the applicability and relevance of improvement strategies like Lean, JIT, TQM, and Six Sigma.
- In the realm of process management, the subsequent step involves directing attention toward attaining the essential objectives of abstraction. These objectives include vertical, horizontal, and aggregate abstractions.

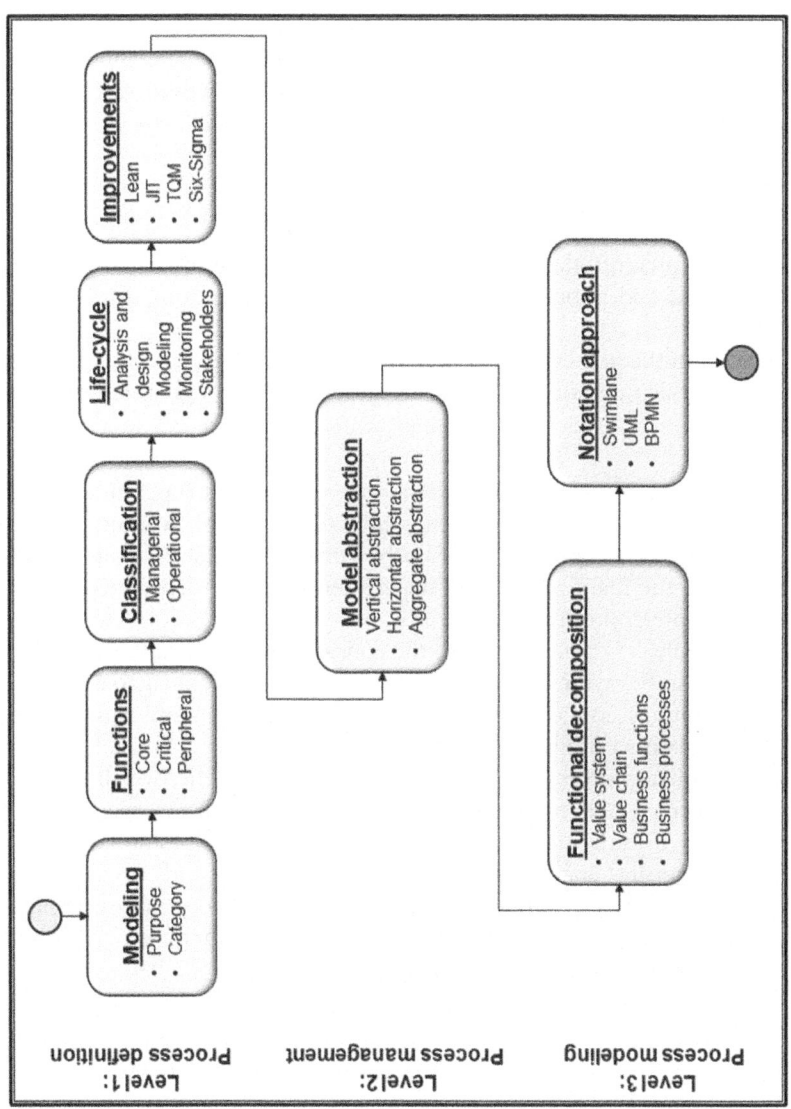

Fig. 6.3 Process flow of business process analysis

- Lastly, the process modeling section encompasses the functional decomposition and places particular emphasis on the modeling process itself. This entails taking into account the organization's value chain, business functions, and processes within its value system. Additionally, the selection of the appropriate notation approach is also considered during this stage.

### 6.3.3   Cost Accounting Process Flow

Figure 6.4 presents the cost accounting process flow model, which has been refined and is built upon the theoretical foundations discussed in Chapter 5.

Similar to the process flow of systems thinking, the process flow of cost accounting also demonstrates the design process through three distinct levels:

- The primary objective is to define the production (operating) environment of the system, which could encompass job costing, process costing, or a combination of both. This objective also entails recognizing the main production departments, service departments, and their interconnectedness.
- Secondly, it is crucial to grasp the concepts of costing and gain clarity on cost behavior. This entails enhancing one's managerial understanding of cost control and recognizing the planning significance associated with different cost categories.
- Finally, it is necessary to recognize and evaluate the overall costing approaches and methods applicable to a particular scenario. This entails considering the practical aspects and informational needs. Additionally, analyzing the potential influence and relevance of supplementary costing concepts, such as the theory of constraints, throughput accounting, lean accounting, and target costing, within a given context could prove beneficial.

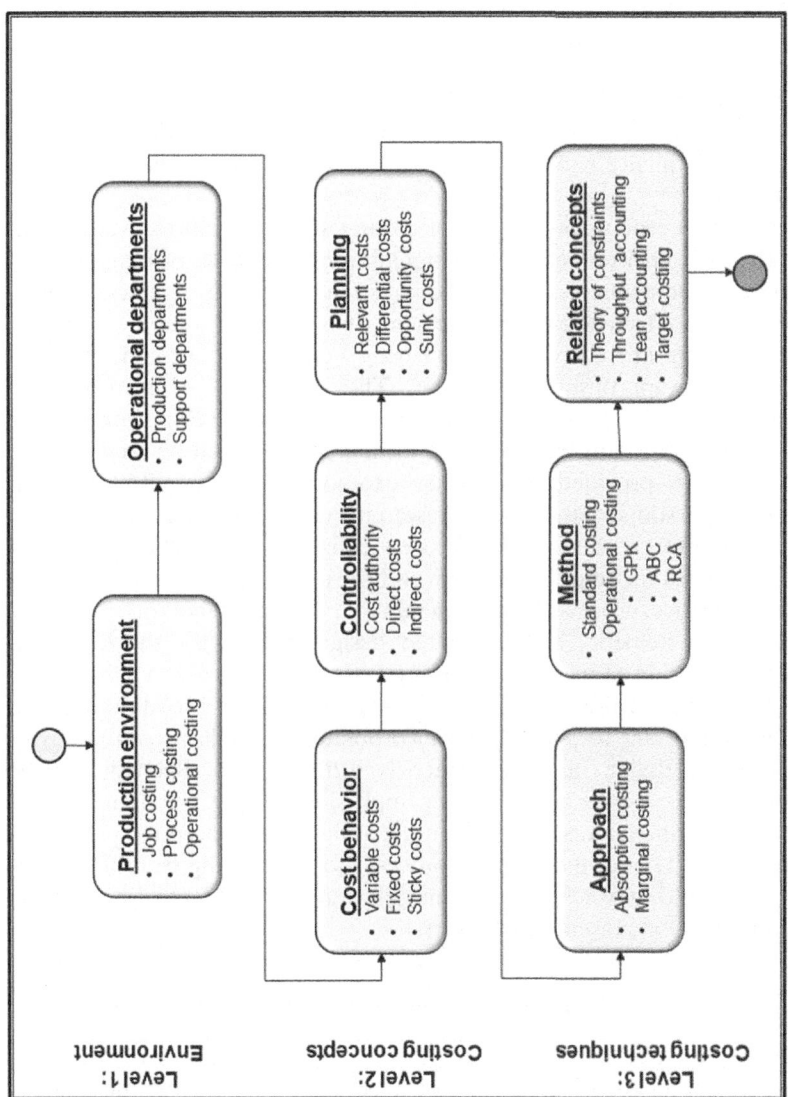

Fig. 6.4   Process flow of cost accounting analysis

## 6.4   Reflection and Learning

The industry experts widely concurred with existing research, given the activities and insights acquired, regarding the significance of managerial costing systems in attaining optimal organizational performance. These systems are acknowledged as vital strategic management tools, even though their potential may be misconstrued or undervalued, due to their distinctive nature compared to standardized financial accounting activities.

Agility is crucial for managerial costing systems to foresee and adjust to dynamic environments. With organizations being intricate and interconnected systems, a systems thinking mindset holds significant value. To achieve effective cost management, it is essential to apply pertinent cost accounting techniques, while having a comprehensive understanding of the relevant business processes. The importance of incorporating the viewpoints of relevant stakeholders for the development of efficient managerial costing systems is evident, as indicated by the literature and insights provided by industry experts. The three-pillar approach provided a sound basis for the research, while the inclusion of knowledgeable experts in the design process enhanced the practical validity of refining both the research problem and the process model. The individual and collective process flows highlighted the importance of a carefully planned, systematic, and integrated design process for the successful implementation of managerial costing systems.

Nevertheless, although the three-pillar concept laid a solid foundation, it was important to address and incorporate these pillars collaboratively during the design of the managerial costing system. Recognizing the organization as a system inherently implies integration among its subsystems and components. Similarly, integrating these conceptual pillars was imperative. Hence, the ultimate process model resulting from these iterations should duly acknowledge and illustrate the conceptual integration and interaction among these pillars.

## 6.5   Formalization of Learning

This ADR stage contributed to the existing knowledge base for practical and academic purposes by formalizing and generalizing the findings obtained from specific iterations. This formalization marked the conclusion of the research, enabling the application of the knowledge in industrial contexts. Within this book, which emphasizes effective managerial costing system design, the process builds upon this stage, serving as a foundation for identifying crucial elements across the three pillars. These elements were then utilized to create *checklists* that support the initial project phases of managerial costing system design and implementation. The following sections provide developmental guides for each pillar.

### 6.5.1   *Systems Thinking Developmental Guide*

The developmental guides for systems thinking are presented in Tables 6.2, 6.3, and 6.4. They aid in identifying, considering, and defining the relevant systems, subsystems, components, relationships, and related aspects within the design process.

### 6.5.2   *Business Processes Developmental Guide*

The final guide for addressing the identification, consideration, and definition of relevant business processes, process levels, and objectives is provided by the business process management developmental guides presented in Tables 6.5, 6.6, and 6.7. These guides were developed through interactions with industry experts during the iteration.

### 6.5.3   *Cost Accounting Developmental Guide*

Tables 6.8, 6.9, and 6.10 present the cost accounting developmental guide, which aids the design process by enabling the identification, consideration, and definition of pertinent cost accounting concepts. This comprehensive guide encompasses suitable costing approaches and methods.

Organizations seeking to enhance their customized managerial costing system could rely on these guides to ensure that vital information requirements and design criteria receive the necessary attention.

## 6.6   In Conclusion

The purpose of this chapter was to validate and enhance the problem by employing the eADR diagnosis iteration within the ADR methodology. The significance and relevance of the managerial costing system

**Table 6.2**   Developmental guide: systems theory

---

**Systems classification**
*Distinguish between contextual system types:*                                    Notes:
* Natural vs Artificial
* Physical vs Conceptual
* Closed vs Open

**System environment**
*Identify and list key aspects:*                                                 Notes:
* Input requirements:
* Output requirements:
* Boundary identification:
* System(s) identification:
* System(s) relationships:
* Sub-system(s) identification:
* Sub-system(s) relationships:

**System design framework**
*Identify system level(s):*                                                      Notes:
* Transcendental system
* Socio-organizational system
* Human system
* Animal system
* Plant system
* Cell and open system
* Cybernetics system
* Simple dynamic system
* Static structural system

*Identify and define relevant building blocks of the components:*                Notes:
Structural components (layout):
Operating components (processing):
Flow components (information):

*Identify and define relevant relationships between components:*                 Notes:
* Symbiotic relationships
* Synergistic relationships
* Redundant relationships

*Define requisite analysis approach(es):*                                        Notes:
* Holistic interactions (Black box)
* Aggregate strata: Subsystems
* Aggregate strata: Components

---

**Table 6.3**   Developmental guide: systems engineering

---

**Application-level considerations**
*Identify application level(s):*                                                    Notes:
                                            Primary        Secondary

* Urban structure
* Communication
* Data and IT
* Healthcare
* Education
* Financial services
* Transportation
* Waste disposal
* Production and construction
* Power generation
* Aerospace and marine

**Application domain considerations**
*Identify application domain(s):*                                                  Notes:
                                            Primary        Secondary

* Large-scale systems
* Small-scale systems
* Newly designed systems
* Complex systems
* Enhancing current systems
* Capital intensive systems
* Supply chain-centric systems
* Governmental or private systems
* Human-modified natural systems

**Methodology considerations**
*Identify and define methodological aspects:*                                      Notes:
* System requirement definitions
* The integrated and holistic design approach
* Interdisciplinary aspects
* Life cycle orientation

---

and the constraints of existing systems were verified through a literature review and insights from industry experts. Three process flow models were created, emphasizing systems thinking, cost accounting, and business processes. These insights were compiled into developmental guides to facilitate the creation of future managerial costing systems. The results obtained from this diagnosis form the foundation for designing an integrated process flow model in the subsequent chapter.

**Table 6.4**   Developmental guide: cybernetics

---

**Goals and objectives**

*Identify and define aspects of the system's feedback loop:*          Notes:
* Sensor(s)
* Control(s)
* Corrective action(s)

*Identify and define aspects of the sub-system's feedback loop:*          Notes:
* Sensor(s)
* Control(s)
* Corrective action(s)

**Managerial considerations**

*Identify and define informational aspects:*          Notes:
* Generation and control
* Life cycle orientation

*Identify and define technological aspects:*          Notes:
* Hardware
* Software
* Internal control

*Identify and define legitimate stakeholders:*          Notes:
* Internal
* External

---

**Table 6.5**   Developmental guide: business process definition

**Process modeling**
*Define the primary purpose of the process model:*                                    Notes:
* Descriptive
* Prescriptive
* Explanatory
*Identify and define the primary activity categories:*                                 Notes:
* Manual activities
* User-interaction activities
* System (back-end) activities
**Process levels**
*Identify and define the functional process categories:*                               Notes:
* Core business processes/functions
* Critical support processes/functions
* Peripheral processes/functions
**Process classification**
*Define the process categorization with respect to the managerial functions:*         Notes:
* Strategic functions and goals
* Business sustainability goals
*Define the process categorization with respect to the operational functions:*        Notes:
* Organizational/interdepartmental functions
* Operational functions
* Implemented/automated functions
**Process life cycle**
*Identify and define the process life cycle objectives:*                               Notes:
* Analysis and design
* Modeling
* Implementation
* Monitoring
* Stakeholder identification
*Identify and define the process improvement applications:*                            Notes:
* Lean manufacturing
* Just-in-time
* Total quality management
* Six Sigma

**Table 6.6**
Developmental guide:
business process
management

| **Model abstraction** | |
| --- | --- |
| *Identify and define the model abstraction objectives:* | Notes: |
| * Vertical abstraction | |
| * Horizontal abstraction | |
| * Aggregate abstraction | |

**Table 6.7**  Developmental guide: business process modeling

---

**Functional decomposition**
*Define the functional decomposition requirements and objectives:*    Notes:
* Value system
* Value chain
* Business functions
* Business processes
**Modeling approaches**
*Identify and define the preferred modeling notation approach:*    Notes:
* Swimlane
* UML
* BPMN

---

**Table 6.8**
Developmental guide:
cost accounting
environment

---

**Costing environment**
*Identify the prevalent production environment:*    Notes:
* Job costing
* Process costing
* Operational costing
*Identify and define the operational departments:*    Notes:
* Production departments
* Support departments

---

**Table 6.9**  Developmental guide: costing concepts

---

**Costing behavior**
*Define prevalent cost behavioral characteristics:*    Notes:
* Variable costs
* Fixed costs
* Sticky costs
**Managerial considerations: Controllability**
*Identify and define cost control characteristics:*    Notes:
* Cost authority
* Direct costs
* Indirect costs
**Managerial considerations: Planning**
*Identify and define the cost concepts in a planning context:*    Notes:
* Relevant costs
* Differential costs
* Opportunity costs
* Sunk costs

---

**Table 6.10**   Developmental guide: cost accounting

| | |
|---|---|
| **Costing approach** | |
| *Identify and define the appropriate costing approach:* | Notes: |
| * Absorption costing | |
| * Marginal costing | |
| **Costing approach** | |
| *Identify and define the appropriate costing approach:* | Notes: |
| * Standard costing | |
| * Operational costing: | |
|   GPK | |
|   ABC | |
|   RCA | |
| **Related concepts** | |
| *Identify and define applicable cost management concepts:* | Notes: |
| * Theory of constraints | |
| * Throughput accounting | |
| * Lean accounting | |
| * Target costing | |

## REFERENCES

Appelbaum, D., Kogan, A., Vasarhelyi, M. and Yan, Z. 2017. Impact of business analytics and enterprise systems on managerial accounting. *International Journal of Accounting Information Systems*, 25:29–44.

Bhaskar, H.L. 2018. Business process reengineering: A process based management tool. *Serbian Journal of Management*, 13(1):63-87.

James, P.C. 2013. An analysis of the factors influencing the adoption of activity-based costing (ABC) in the financial sector in Jamaica. *International Journal of Business and Social Research*, 3(7):8–18.

Labro, E. 2019. Costing systems. *Foundations and Trends in Accounting*, 13(3–4):267–404. https://doi.org/10.1561/1400000058.

Mullarkey, M. and Hevner, A. 2018. An elaborated action design research process model. *European Journal of Information Systems*, 28(1):6-20.

Rogerson, C. and Scott, E. 2014. Motivating an action design research approach to implementing online training in an organisational context. *Interactive Technology and Smart Education*, 11(1):32–44. https://doi.org/10.1108/ITSE-10-2013-0026

Sein, M.K., Henfridsson, O, Purao, S., Rossi, M. and Lindgren, R. 2011. Action design research. *MIS Quarterly*, 35(1):37–56.

# CHAPTER 7

# Second eADR Iteration: Solution Integration

The previous chapter developed process flow models and managerial costing systems design guides. This chapter will build on the objective of integrating process flows integrating organizational systems and complexities in process flows. The guiding principles of the chosen methodology will be briefly contextualized against the current object-centric design iteration. The chapter will then document design activities, including problem reiteration, artifact building, intervention, evaluation, and outcome reflection, followed by formalization of what has been learned in context.

## 7.1 Guiding Principles of the Design Iteration

The object-centric design iteration involves multiple cycles of discussion and refinement of aspects such as artifact features, requirements, and implementation needs. This is illustrated in Fig. 7.1.

In alignment with the overall methodology, the four ADR stages and the seven guiding principles within the iterative eADR cycles are explained in context in Table 7.1.

Contextualizing the solution design in an ADR context involves a holistic approach, combining problem-solving, design thinking, and research methodologies with input from practitioners as a reality check for the solution The ADR approach empowers the organization's design

© The Author(s), under exclusive license to Springer Nature          131
Singapore Pte Ltd. 2024
P. W. Buys, *Crafting Efficiency in Managerial Costing System Design*,
https://doi.org/10.1007/978-981-97-0934-2_7

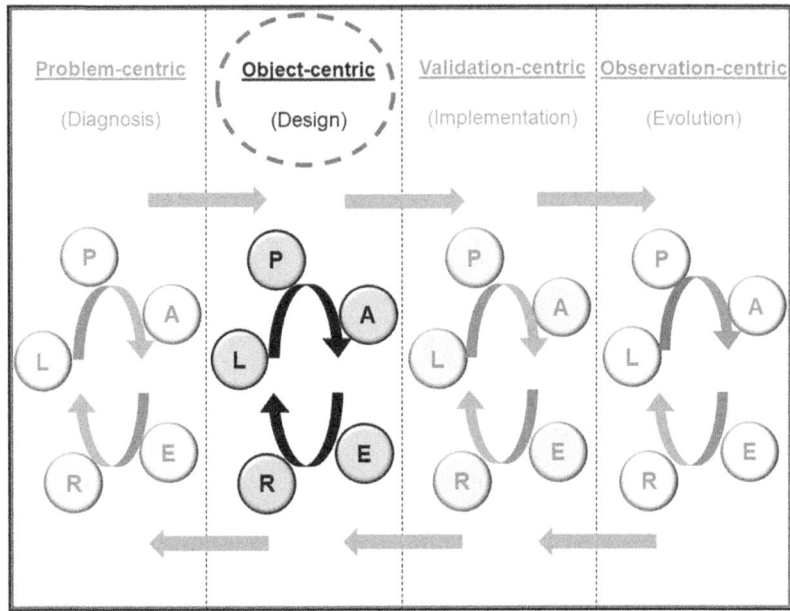

**Fig. 7.1**  Object-centric eADR design iteration

team iteratively and contributes to academic knowledge and practical business outcomes. The following sections will detail the sequential execution of the stages mentioned.

## 7.2  PROBLEM FORMULATION

### 7.2.1  *Problem Contextualization*

This book emphasizes the significance of practice-inspired research in generating practical knowledge for specific problems. This book originated from the observation that managerial costing systems often prioritize external financial reporting, relegating effective cost management to a secondary role. This assertion is supported by various literary sources, including Appelbaum et al. (2017), Labro (2019), Tsai et al. (2015), and Van der Stede (2017). Manufacturing is a crucial industry in global economies (Stocker et al. 2017; Mdluli et al. 2019). The industry

**Table 7.1** Design activities

| ADR stages and principles | | Key activities of the current iteration |
| --- | --- | --- |
| **Stage 1:**<br>Problem formulation | **Principle 1:**<br>Practice-inspired research | Practice-inspired: Confirming the research problem's validity, drawing from the literature review, and obtaining input from industry experts during the problem diagnosis phase |
| | **Principle 2:**<br>Theory-ingrained artifact | Theory-ingrained: Reemphasizing the theoretical foundation by approaching managerial costing systems within a systems thinking context |
| | | Dimensional integration: Refining the above by integrating costing processes and operational and costing systems |
| **Stage 2:**<br>Building, intervention, and evaluation | **Principle 3:**<br>Reciprocal shaping | Following the integration, the process model's BIE activities were carried out iteratively with relevant industry experts, involving: |
| | **Principle 4**<br>Mutually influential roles | • analyzing the identified dimensions to explain in detail the system levels within each; and |
| | **Principle 5:**<br>Authentic and concurrent evaluation | • defining and designing a process flow model based on a multilevel dimensional process |
| | | (continued) |

**Table 7.1** (continued)

| ADR stages and principles | | Key activities of the current iteration |
|---|---|---|
| **Stage 3:**<br>Reflection and learning | **Principle 6:**<br>Guided emergence | The notes and feedback from researcher–practitioner interactions were the foundation for reflecting on acquired knowledge and for guiding efforts to generalize the outcomes |
| **Stage 4:**<br>Formalization of learning | **Principle 7:** Generalized outcomes | A contextual managerial costing system environment was formulated, taking into account critical considerations within each dimension of the problem class |

experts involved in this project validated the importance of cost management in organizational and performance management in this industry. They also noted the relevance of stakeholders concerning contemporary social and environmental responsibilities. Additionally, they expressed that improving organizational performance often takes a backseat to external reporting objectives and outdated organizational requirements that shape managerial costing systems.

The proposed three-pillar approach was recognized as a solid foundation for managerial costing system design. The industry experts affirmed that adopting a systems thinking approach would lead to a more integrated way of designing managerial costing systems, moving away from traditional linear reporting objectives. Understanding true costs is crucial for effective decision-making, and a well-maintained managerial costing system generates relevant information for supporting decision-making, contributing significantly to the organization's value creation objectives. Systems thinking enables a broader view of organizational functions, supporting a well-structured managerial costing system design. Business processes and functions were acknowledged by the industry experts as being integral to organizational operations and essential in selecting and refining cost accounting methods and approaches, directly impacting managerial information.

### 7.2.2    Dimensional Integration

The knowledge and concepts from the first iteration were integrated to refine the complex nature of the problem of designing effective managerial costing systems. This integration, shown in Fig. 7.2, helps understand the overall problem along the dimensions of costing processes, operational systems, and costing systems.

As shown in the Fig. 7.2, integrating the initial three-pillar concept gave rise to the focus dimensions of costing processes, operational systems, and costing systems. For our purposes, these dimensions are considered as follows:

- Costing processes: The first dimension combines conceptual aspects from the business process and cost accounting pillars. It has three levels, i.e., understanding strategic (financial) management requirements and objectives from the high-level organizational systems perspective, considering midtier financial management subsystems,

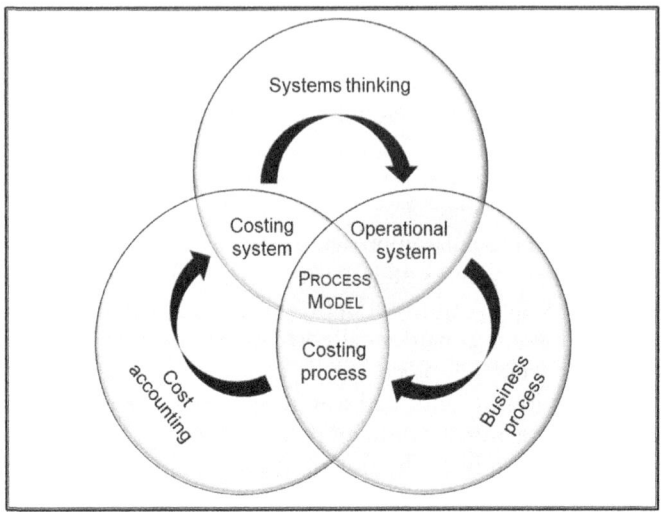

**Fig. 7.2** Conceptual integration

and acknowledging low-level cost management component-level realities that support cost management. Two perspectives hereto should be considered:

- The function of costing involves business processes, which encompass cost accounting activities. While these activities are often associated with the accounting or finance department, we argue that they should be viewed and executed in a broader context. In a manufacturing environment, many costing-related activities may occur in technical and production areas, such as product design, bill-of-material formulation, and production planning. Furthermore, stakeholders external to the organization may influence and be influenced by the applied costing processes.
- It is essential to recognize that business processes or activities significantly contribute to cost incurrence, aligning with the arguments supporting operations-centric costing methods. The overview of cost accounting perspectives (Chapter 5) briefly identified three such methods: (i) GPK, which adopts

a marginal costing approach to emphasize accurate operational modeling (Okutmus 2015); (ii) ABC, which, following a similar vein, uses a full costing approach to analyze operational activities (Alami and ElMaraghy 2020); and (iii) RCA, which highlights that operational activities lead to the consumption of organizational resources (Okutmus 2015). Therefore, within the context of the costing processes dimension, GPK, ABC, and RCA share similar philosophical foundations, emphasizing the significance of business processes in a cost accounting context.

- Operational systems: Optimum resource management and utilization are complex managerial activities. Rosin et al. (2021) state that integrated operational systems require decentralized decisions for consistent optimization. In this second dimension, organizations are seen as dynamic systems operating in complex environments where managers, cost accountants, and engineers analyze the realities affecting the organizations. Operational systems are the cohesive units that bind various operational aspects and incorporate an organizational systems perspective in identifying, analyzing, and evaluating business processes. Multiple management analyses and aggregation levels exist considering the broad view of costing processes. The operational systems dimension integrates the systems thinking and business process pillars, divided into three levels: high-level organizational value system analysis, midlevel value chain functional analysis, and low-level detailed process analysis. While a bottom-up managerial costing system design may be logical, we propose an initial top-down approach to gain a comprehensive understanding of the organizational environment before conducting a detailed operational activity analysis.
- Costing systems: According to Labro (2019), costing systems involve costing processes for the measurement of costs, but for our purposes, we extended this definition to include management and decision support objectives in cost measurement. Costing systems recognize the role of systems thinking in cost accounting. When designing managerial costing systems, cost information is needed for various purposes, such as budgeting, decision-making, cost management, inventory valuation, management control, and performance management. Given an organization's inherent operational complexity, having diverse subsystems and goals, a top-down

approach is proposed to consider relevant cost accounting aspects. This involves a broad-based requirements analysis of cost behavior characteristics and management requirements, and the selection of appropriate costing approaches. An example is target costing, setting the selling price based on market affordability, in contrast to the conventional cost-plus approach. The high-level aspect in context is thus the overall manufacturing environment of the organizational system, followed by a midlevel analysis of cost behavior and applicable costing approaches. The specific costing methods are decided upon only at the final low-level dimensional analysis.

As set out in this section, the refinement and dimensional integration of the research problem in a context formed the foundation for the subsequent building, intervention, and evaluation stages, which will be detailed in the next section.

## 7.3   Building, Intervention, and Evaluation

The multidimensional design perspective of the integrated process flow considers the integrated dimensions. The multilevel analysis is based on aggregate-level analysis, involving black box analysis, (sub)system analysis, and component analysis interactions. Figure 7.3 presents an overview of the process flow resulting from researcher–practitioner team interactions.

The process flow illustrated in the Fig. 7.3 is explained in Table 7.2. The specific objectives within each dimensional level are also detailed.

## 7.4   Reflection and Learning

This stage reflects on the activities, outcomes, and knowledge gained from this design iteration. It integrated the three-pillar concept, derived from academic literature and input from the current cohort of industry experts who emphasized the relevance and importance of management costing systems in driving value creation objectives, into the three dimensions of costing processes, operational systems, and costing systems.

One critical issue is recognizing the complexity of effective managerial costing systems. The industry experts also emphasized complexities

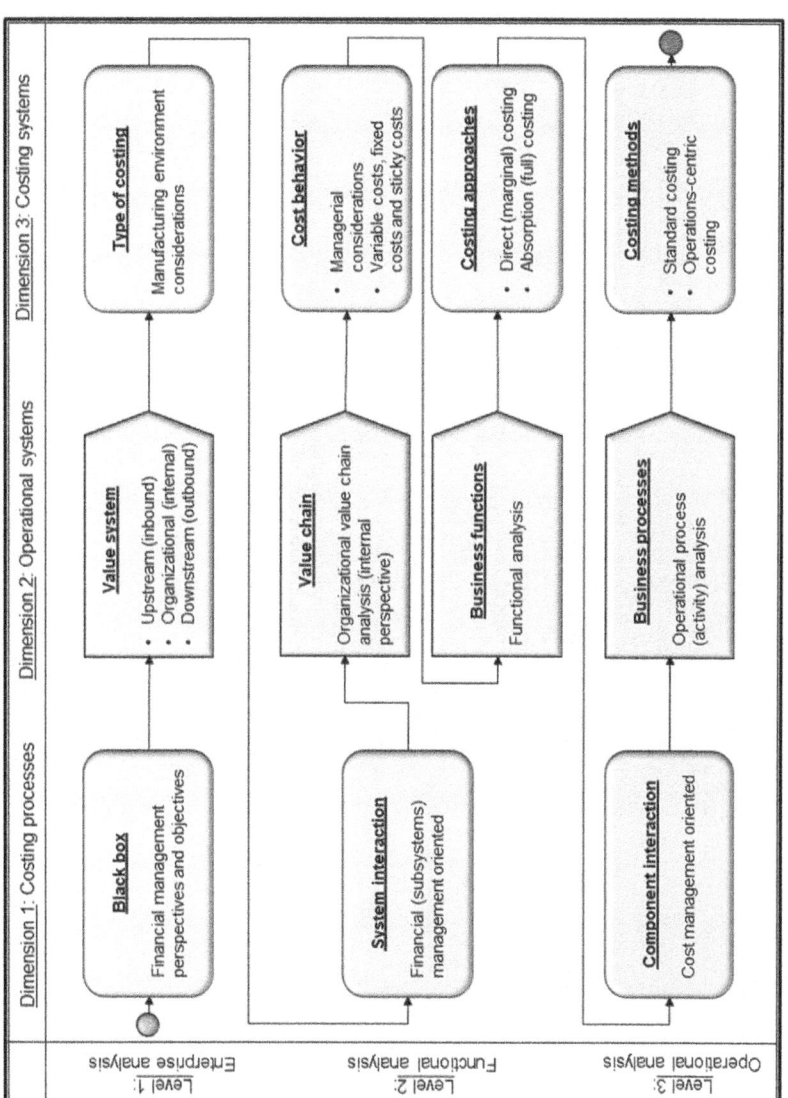

**Fig. 7.3** Integrated process flow

**Table 7.2** Multilevel dimensional costing process analysis

**Level 1: Enterprise level:** Enterprise analysis focuses on high-level implications for effective cost management, emphasizing organizational impact rather than intricate costing methods

| | | |
|---|---|---|
| **Black box:** The foundational starting point of the process flow is a holistic reflection on the broader organizational value system. The focus should be on effective financial management and understanding the objectives of the managerial costing system in its specific scenario. This reflection aligns with the organization's strategies, mission, and vision, aiming to understand its role as both a consumer and generator of management information within the overall value system | **Value system:** The process flow comes closer to the organization's business realities, and analyzing the organizational value stream is crucial for cost management initiatives. The value system considerations include (i) an inbound value stream analysis that considers external stakeholders, such as investors, financial resource providers, and suppliers, as their activities can impact the organization's costs; (ii) an internal value stream analysis as a high-level organizational analysis with a focus on sound financial management; and (iii) an outbound value stream analysis that focuses on external stakeholders that may influence the organization's financial management and related cost management activities | **Type of costing:** The focus shifts to the operational production environment where the manufacturing activities take place. Before designing a sound managerial costing system, it is essential to clarify the basis of job, process, or operational (hybrid) costing in the context of the actual manufacturing environment |

**Level 2: Functional level:** Functional analysis focuses on understanding the organizational system and related interactions

**(Sub)system interaction:** The focus is on the functions and interactions of financial subsystems. It is crucial to know which financial systems are in use (or should be) and to understand their capabilities. For analyzing the costing processes, it is vital that the various subsystems can relate and integrate seamlessly. In the context of analyzing the costing processes, it is vital that the various subsystems can relate and integrate

**Value chain:** The initial second-level operational systems analysis centers on the organizational value chain, focusing on the functions of different business units from a cost management standpoint. It involves analyzing and understanding operational business functions, considering Porter's *Value Chain Analysis*, and identifying primary production and secondary support departments

**Business functions:** After understanding the cost behavior characteristics, the second iteration of operational analysis delves into a detailed functional analysis of activities within business functions. A further objective is identifying the most suitable basis and method for allocating the support departments' costs to the main production departments

**Cost behavior:** Once the high-level operational functions and interactions are understood, the initial costing systems investigation can begin. Within this context, the first key aspect is to clarify the management objectives of planning and control, which will also influence decisions regarding cost allocation approaches. A second analysis objective is to understand the cost behavior within the various functions, distinguishing between fixed costs, variable costs, and sticky costs. This understanding will directly impact later cost accounting activities, including clarifying production volumes for planning and cost allocation and allocating the basis of the support departments' costs

**Costing approaches:** The choice between direct (marginal) and absorption (full) costing depends on the managerial costing system's ultimate objective. Direct costing is the best option for supporting internal managerial decisions and achieving long-term value creation and economic viability objectives. However, if the managerial costing system needs to provide information for external reporting purposes, an absorption costing approach is seen as the appropriate choice

(continued)

**Table 7.2** (continued)

**Level 3: Operational level:** Operational analysis focuses on practical cost management

| | | |
|---|---|---|
| **Component interaction:** In the last analysis level, the costing processes dimension involves understanding cost management and other related functions from a system components perspective. The focus is on identifying and analyzing specific requirements within the specific context, such as how cost information may need to be used in budgeting, planning, or supporting controlling activities | **Business processes:** In the last operational analysis level, the focus is on actual process mapping (value stream mapping), involving selecting the most suitable process modeling technique (for example, swimlane, UML, or BPMN) based on the organization's user requirements and technological infrastructure capabilities (*The purpose of mapping the business processes is to identify detailed activities, enabling the identification and possible elimination of nonvalue-adding activities and streamlining processes. This analysis should support the final selection and justification of the most appropriate costing method.*) | **Costing methods:** Through completing the previous analyses, the organizational system has been well contextualized and understood, and the costing method is decided on. The configuration of the selected costing method then begins |

related to revenue streams, product design, life cycle, industry characteristics, and workforce characteristics. Manufacturing environments are inherently complex, having diverse and unique processes, inputs and outputs, and nonstandardizable requirements leading to hesitancy in designing effective managerial costing systems. However, the systematic approach facilitated by eADR/ADR should help identify, address, and preempt potential issues, alleviating complexity and making effective managerial costing systems achievable.

Regarding costing approaches, the participating industry experts proposed an additional discretionary (target) costing approach, initially following a cost leadership approach, allowing revenue and market share growth while recovering lost margin in after-sales services and future add-on offerings. Furthermore, the industry experts reiterated the complexity of and multiple options in cost accounting, including standard costing, operations-centric approaches, throughput accounting, and lean costing. Notwithstanding the chosen costing approach or method, understanding the integrated nature of the organization's operational systems, objectives, and value creation goals remains crucial.

## 7.5   Formalization of Learning

The fourth stage of ADR aims to formalize the design iteration knowledge within the broader problem class. This formalization is intended to contribute to practical knowledge. With the current eADR iteration still under development, the knowledge gained highlights the complexity and integrated nature of the managerial costing system and its operating environment.

The design process considered three key points: (i) the organizational system operates within a complex environment with various stakeholders; (ii) effective managerial costing systems require a holistic systems approach; and (iii) business processes influence the application of cost accounting techniques, and vice versa. Therefore, in formalizing the learning, the process model will be defined within a contextual managerial costing system environment, as shown in Fig. 7.4.

The managerial costing system environment considers both inbound and outbound value streams, acknowledging the impact of external forces. The process model should also consider inbound stakeholders as feeders and outbound stakeholders as consumers of the system's product. Within the internal environment, the three integrated dimensions (costing

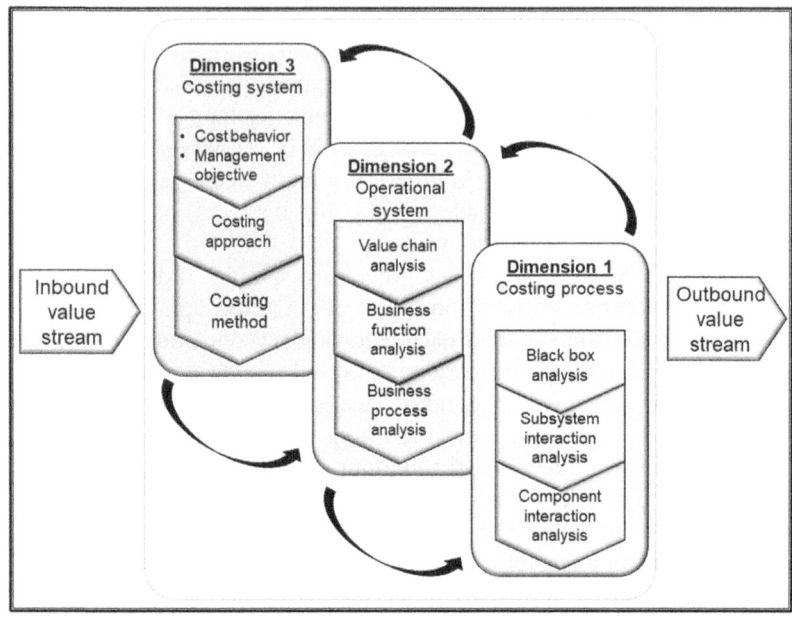

**Fig. 7.4**   Contextual managerial costing environmental

processes, operational systems, and costing systems) form the detailed basis of the system's components, subcomponents, and relationships. The pertinent aggregate-level analysis within these dimensions must also be considered. The design activities within the process model may move between specific dimension boundaries within these aggregate levels, following a sequential pattern based on the analysis levels in the earlier process flow.

## 7.6   CHAPTER SUMMARY

The objective of this chapter was to illustrate the design aspects of the process model based on the book's primary objective. This iteration integrated the three-pillar concept into a three-dimensional understanding. The researcher–practitioner team revisited the outcomes of the diagnosis iteration, refining the process flow through the dimensions of costing processes, operational systems, and costing systems with increasing levels of depth. In this context, the first level focuses on understanding the organization's fit in its value stream, the second level on functional processes, and the third level on detailed operations. A contextual managerial costing system environment model was created to represent various aspects of the process model.

In the next chapter, the building blocks from this design iteration will be verified and validated, refining the process model through collaboration with the next cohort of relevant industry participants.

## References

Alami, D. and ElMaraghy, W. 2020. Traditional and activity based aggregate job costing model. *53rd CIRP Conference on Manufacturing Systems 2020*, Chicago, IL.

Appelbaum, D., Kogan, A., Vasarhelyi, M. and Yan, Z. 2017. Impact of business analytics and enterprise systems on managerial accounting. *International Journal of Accounting Information Systems*, 25:29–44.

Labro, E. 2019. Costing systems. *Foundations and Trends in Accounting*, 13(3–4):267–404. https://doi.org/10.1561/1400000058.

Mdluli, P., Mncayi, P. and Mc Camel, T. 2019. *Examining factors that drive government spending in South Africa*. IISES Intentional Academic Conference, Barcelona. https://doi.org/10.20472/IAC.2019.052.037.

Okutmus, E. 2015. Resource consumption accounting with cost dimension and an application in a glass factory. *International Journal of Academic Research in Accounting, Finance and Management Sciences*, 5(1):46–57.

Rosin, F., Forget, P., Lamouri, S. and Pellerin, R. 2021. Impact of Industry 4.0 on decision-making in an operational context. *Advances in Production Engineering & Management*, 16(4):500–514.

Stocker, M., Lakatos, C., Ohnsorge, F. and Kose, M.A. 2017. Understanding the global role of the U.S. economy. https://voxeu.org/article/understanding-global-role-us-economy Date of access: 21 July 2018.

Tsai, W.H., Tsaur, T., Chou, Y., Liu, J., Hsu, J. and Hsieh, C. 2015. Integrating the activity-based costing system and life-cycle assessment into green decision-making. *International Journal of Production Research*, 53(2):451–465.

Van der Stede, W.A. 2017. "Global" management accounting research: Some reflections. *Journal of International Accounting Research*, 16(2):1–8.

# CHAPTER 8

# Third eADR Iteration: Solution Validation

The preceding chapters detailed the design process of the process model, involving problem-centric diagnosis and object-centric design iterations. This chapter seeks to validate the process model with system design experts. Like was done for the previous iterations ADR-related activities, such as problem formulation, building, intervention, evaluation, reflection, and outcome formalization, will be documented.

## 8.1 Guiding Principles of the Implementation Iteration

In the validation-centric implementation iteration, a primary goal is to enhance previously designed artifact(s) from earlier iterations (Mullarkey and Hevner 2019). This refinement process involves verifying adherence to the design requirements and validating the artifact's fitness for purpose. Figure 8.1 illustrates the iteration's contextual fit.

The composition of the researcher–practitioner team changed for this iteration. As detailed earlier in Chapter 2, industry experts with experience in managerial costing systems design and implementation contributed to the validation. Table 8.1 explains the application of each ADR principle within the context of this iteration.

© The Author(s), under exclusive license to Springer Nature     147
Singapore Pte Ltd. 2024
P. W. Buys, *Crafting Efficiency in Managerial Costing System Design*,
https://doi.org/10.1007/978-981-97-0934-2_8

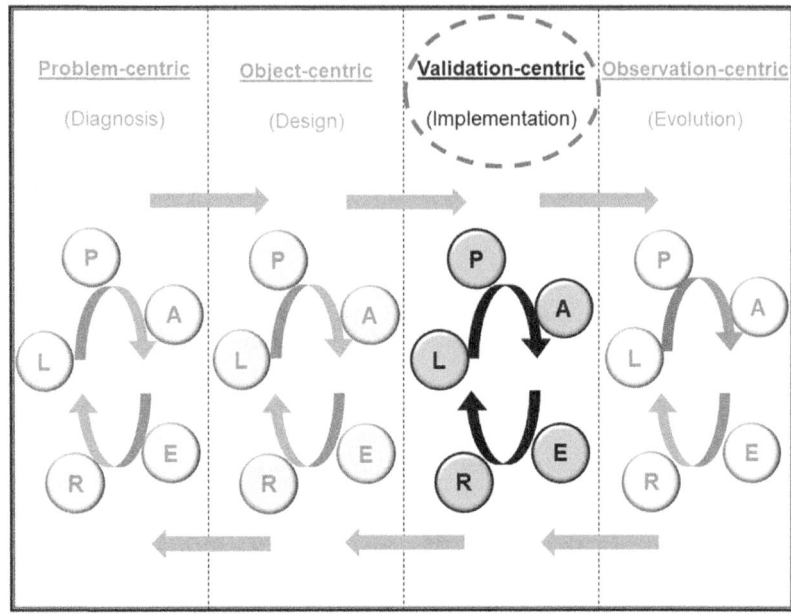

**Fig. 8.1**  Validation-centric eADR implementation iteration

The verification and validation process began by introducing the problem and objectives to the new cohort of industry experts. Subsequently, they were provided with the supportive artifacts from earlier iterations, i.e., contextual system environment model, developmental guides, and process flow. A five-point Likert scale (Bryman and Bell 2014) was used to evaluate the artifacts against predefined design statements, according to (1) Strongly agree, (2) Agree, (3) Undecided, (4) Disagree, (5) Strongly disagree. Responses of either *Strongly agree* or *Agree* were considered adequate adherence to the design statements.

Each design statement targeted a distinct deliverable according to the eADR process:

- Verification design statements: To verify adherence to appropriate design criteria, the following five conceptual design statements were presented to the industry experts:

**Table 8.1** Implementation activities

| ADR stages and principles | | Key activities of the current iteration |
|---|---|---|
| **Stage 1:** Problem formulation | **Principle 1:** Practice-inspired research | The topic's significance and relevance were considered in the context of: |
| | **Principle 2:** Theory-ingrained artifact | • the intricate practicality of designing effective managerial costing systems; and |
| | | • the theoretical foundation of addressing managerial costing system design within a systems thinking framework |
| | | Verification and validation tasks confirmed: |
| | | • the relevance of the problem and objectives within context; and |
| | | • the effectiveness of the integrated three-pillar approach in solving this problem |
| **Stage 2:** Building, intervention, and evaluation | **Principle 3:** Reciprocal shaping | Evaluated against specified design criteria, the supporting elements for the final model's verification included: |
| | **Principle 4:** Mutually influential roles | • suitability of the contextual system environment; |
| | **Principle 5:** Authentic and concurrent evaluation | • suitability of the developmental guides; and |
| | | • suitability of the process flow representation |

(continued)

**Table 8.1** (continued)

| ADR stages and principles | | Key activities of the current iteration |
|---|---|---|
| **Stage 3:**<br>Reflection and learning | **Principle 6:**<br>Guided emergence | The feedback from researcher–practitioner interactions was the foundation for reflecting on acquired knowledge |
| **Stage 4:**<br>Formalization of learning | **Principle 7:**<br>Generalized outcomes | Considering the problem class and the specified design criteria, the following was achieved:<br>• verification of the suggested process model's efficacy in enabling effective managerial costing system design; and<br>• validation of the suggested process model's contribution to effective managerial costing system design |

- *Verification design statement # 1*: The research problem and objective align with the contemporary manufacturing industry's needs for efficient managerial costing system design.
- *Verification design statement # 2*: Project team members at the relevant team levels can comprehend the contextual system environment to ensure comprehensive design perspectives.
- *Verification design statement # 3*: Project team members at various levels can interpret and apply the developmental guides to fulfill essential information requirements.
- *Verification design statement # 4*: Project team members can understand and implement the process flow to meet crucial functional design prerequisites.
- *Verification design statement # 5*: The process model should enable effective managerial costing systems design.

• Validation design statements: Regarding validating the intended functionality of the final process model, the industry experts were presented with the following two conceptual design statements:

- *Validation design statement # 1*: The initial three-pillar approach, expanded into the costing process, operational system, and costing system dimensions, is a pertinent and supportive basis for the resulting process model.
- *Validation design statement # 2*: The integrated process model should aid in designing effective managerial costing systems.

## 8.2   PROBLEM FORMULATION

The book emphasizes the value of practice-inspired research for creating supportive knowledge to address particular issues. While designing effective managerial costing systems, the industry experts from the diagnosis and design iterations echoed published research findings by highlighting that managerial costing systems are often (i) of secondary significance in financial systems design, (ii) integrated into systems for external financial reporting, and (iii) crucial for practical and effective management functions.

We detailed our suggested three-pillar managerial costing system design method to provide the project's context to the industry experts involved in the current iteration. This approach employs systems thinking from relevant literature to achieve an all-encompassing organizational perspective. Additionally, a business process outlook recognizes the significance of real-world operational aspects in determining and enhancing cost accounting methods. The further amalgamation of the three-pillar notion led to the dimensions of (i) costing processes, which align the conceptual elements from business processes and cost accounting; (ii) operational systems, which integrate operational aspects into a functional unit; and (iii) costing systems, which combine systems thinking and cost accounting pillars.

While the aforementioned was iteratively validated by the industry experts in the first and second iterations, additional confirmation of topic relevance and solution suitability was sought from the industry experts in the current iteration, focusing on implementation perspectives. In addressing the complex issue surrounding the design of effective managerial costing systems, the current-iteration industry experts validated the research problem and objective against the first verification design statement, as shown in Table 8.2.

The experts were requested to affirm that the three foundational pillars (conceptual) aid in comprehending the cost management challenge. This evaluation involved assessing the resulting integration within the framework of the first validation design statement, as shown in Table 8.3.

Thus, from the feedback, this panel of industry experts reaffirmed the problem's relevance and the fundamental research groundwork.

**Table 8.2**   First verification design statement

| | |
|---|---|
| **Design statement** | The research problem and objective align with the contemporary manufacturing industry's need for efficient managerial costing system design |
| **Response** | *Agree* and *Strongly agree* |
| **Notes** | One expert mentioned that, as design and implementation specialists, they might not be directly involved in manufacturing industry management decisions, yet their role provides insight into client perceptions and the book's topical significance |
| | Another expert highlighted that they had crafted and implemented their own managerial costing system owing to the inadequacy of off-the-shelf solutions for meeting their needs |

**Table 8.3**   First validation design statement

| | |
|---|---|
| **Design statement** | The initial three-pillar approach, expanded into costing process, operational system, and costing system dimensions, is a pertinent and supportive basis for the resulting process model |
| **Response** | *Agree* and *Strongly agree* |
| **Notes** | There was a recognized understanding of the intricate and interwoven nature of cost management endeavors and organizational management complexity |
| | Unlike the response to the preceding verification design statement, the design and implementation experts demonstrated a more profound recognition of system design's intricate, integrated nature and expressed varied viewpoints rather than solely acknowledging the book's topical relevance |

## 8.3   Building, Intervention, and Evaluation

This stage centered on verifying the artifacts crafted in prior iterations against the design statements. Thus, the artifacts were anticipated to remain essentially unchanged, other than some conceptual enhancements. To clarify this sequential rationale outlined in the corresponding eADR iterations, consider the following:

- In the *diagnosis* iteration, the three-pillar concept within developmental guides emerged from individual process flows.
- In the *design* iteration, the contextual system environment model arose from the process flow of that iteration.

As vital building blocks for the design of effective managerial costing systems, a practical verification process model should arguably sequentially address these components: (i) contextual system environment model; (ii) developmental guides; and (iii) process flow, as will be outlined in the next section.

### 8.3.1   Verification of the Contextual System Environment Model

The purpose of verifying the comprehensive design perspectives shown in the contextual system environment model is to empower stakeholders in managerial costing system design to comprehend the conceptual significance, role, and function of cost management within an effective management framework, as follows:

- It is vital to note that cost management operates within the broader organizational value stream, encompassing both inbound and outbound value streams.
- Consequently, the managerial costing system is not confined to internal operations; it involves different levels and dimensions within the organization's functions, as well as interacts with the inputs and outputs of the system.

The industry experts accepted the contextual system environment model against the second verification design statement to affirm this aspect of the proposed process model, as shown in Table 8.4.

Following the mentioned suggestion, the presentation of the managerial costing system's contextual environment model was revised to a left-to-right format for improved readability. Figure 8.2 depicts this verified contextual system environment after this adaptation.

Essentially unchanged, the verified contextual system environment model still depicts cost management's consideration of external forces via inbound and outbound value streams. The model acknowledges the significance of external stakeholders, acknowledging inbound stakeholders as contributors and outbound stakeholders as consumers, both influencing effective cost management. Additionally, the internal environment consists of integrated dimensions: costing processes, operational

**Table 8.4**  Second verification design statement

| | |
|---|---|
| **Design statement** | Project team members at the relevant team levels can comprehend the contextual system environment to ensure comprehensive design perspectives |
| **Response** | *Agree* and *Strongly agree* |
| **Notes** | Confirmed the need for the managerial costing system to incorporate multiple stakeholders, embrace holistic systems thinking, and recognize the interplay between business processes and cost accounting methods |
| | The industry experts underscored the significance of perceiving the system within the broader value stream, considering external inbound and outbound stakeholders |
| | A suggestion was made to consider a left-to-right visual presentation instead of the existing right-to-left format |

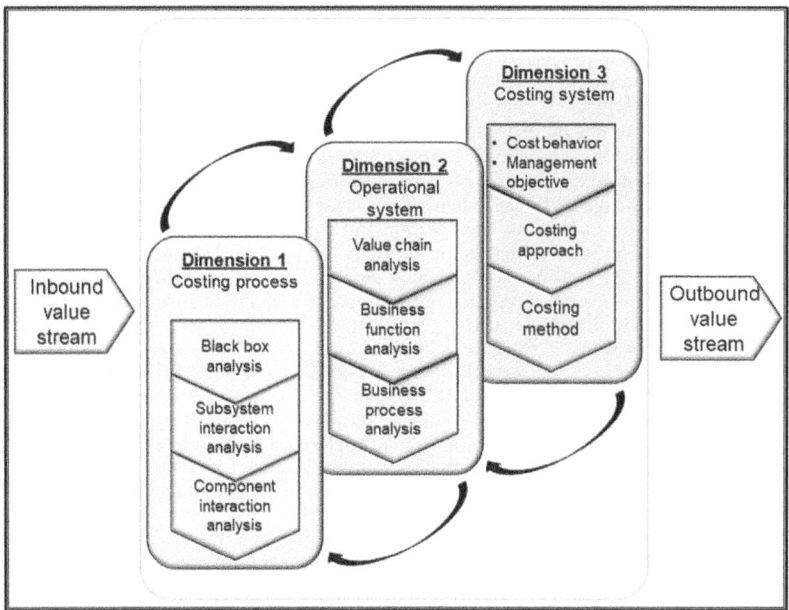

**Fig. 8.2** Verified contextual managerial costing system environment model

systems, and costing systems. These dimensions underpin the system's components, subcomponents, and relationships, and thus detailed analysis at an aggregate level within these dimensions remains crucial. Analysis at an aggregate level within these dimensions remains crucial. Design actions may transition between dimension boundaries at aggregate levels, following a sequential pattern based on analysis levels.

### 8.3.2 Verification of the Developmental Guides

Verification of vital information needs, supported by developmental guides, centers on the quality of data employed in managerial costing system design. Initial developmental guides, crafted for each pillar through interactions with the first- and second-iteration industry experts and process flows, aimed to ensure precise information collection. Completeness and contextual relevance are crucial to guaranteeing effective information acquisition. Extending from the contextual managerial

**Table 8.5**    Third verification design statement

| | |
|---|---|
| **Design statement** | Project team members at various levels can interpret and apply the developmental guides to fulfill essential information requirements |
| **Response** | Consensus on *Strongly agree* (with a proviso) |
| **Notes** | While aligning with the design statement, a concern was raised about the potential challenge of crafting suitable developmental guides. On one side, each organizational system's uniqueness might raise uncertainty regarding the comprehensive identification and consideration of all pertinent aspects, making standardized guides challenging. Conversely, concerns emerged that the existing developmental guides could appear overly complex, and doubts were expressed about the necessity of specific managerial costing system design concepts |
| | Consequently, the developmental guides underwent review, leading to a simplified structure and reduced data collection requisites, particularly in the systems thinking pillar. The guides were streamlined, eliminating contextually irrelevant considerations, such as different system types, some system-level categories, and some application domain levels |
| | Moreover, while the high-level considerations across the three dimensions aimed for comprehensiveness, an option to include supplementary notes was introduced within each dimension |
| | It was suggested that these guides be integrated into a software application with drill-down functionality, linking to supplementary notes and information. The enhanced developmental guides and accompanying notes are outlined in Tables 8.6, 8.7, 8.8, 8.9, 8.10, and 8.11 |

costing system environment, the facet of completeness systematically identifies and addresses all pivotal aspects of the managerial costing system. Empowering the system design team, the facet of relevance ensures the assessment, collection, and sourcing of all relevant supportive information for developing the intended managerial costing system. The present industry experts assessed the third verification design statement regarding information acquisition, as summarized in Table 8.5.

### *8.3.3    Process Flow Verification*

This artifact aims to visually depict design sequences for creating an efficient managerial costing system to confirm the functional design requisites of the integrated process flow. The process flow amalgamates earlier artifacts within the process model hierarchy, integrating design insights from the contextual system environment model and developmental guides. With regard to the verification of this process flow, the current-iteration

**Table 8.6**  Systems thinking developmental guide

| Systems theory | Systems engineering | Cybernetics |
| --- | --- | --- |
| **Identify key environmental aspects**<br>* Input requirements<br>* Output requirements<br>* System boundary<br>* Key components<br>* Key component relationships<br>* Key subsystems<br>* Key subsystem relationships<br>**Design framework: System levels**<br>* Socio-organizational system<br>* Cybernetic system<br>* Simple dynamic system<br>* Static structural system<br>**Define the building blocks: Components**<br>* Structural components (layout)<br>* Operating components (processing)<br>* Flow components (information)<br>**Define the relationships: Components**<br>* Symbiotic relationships<br>* Synergistic relationships<br>* Redundant relationships<br>**Refine the requisite analysis approach**<br>* Holistic interactions (black box)<br>* Aggregate strata: Subsystems<br>* Aggregate strata: Components | **Define application level**<br>* Urban structures<br>* Communications<br>* Data and ICT<br>* Healthcare<br>* Education<br>* Financial services<br>* Transportation<br>* Waste disposal<br>* Power generation<br>* Aerospace and marine<br>**Define application domain**<br>* Large-scale systems<br>* Small-scale systems<br>* Newly designed systems<br>* Complex systems<br>* System enhancement<br>* Supply chain-centric systems<br>* Public systems<br>* Private systems<br>**Consider methodology considerations**<br>* Systems requirement definitions<br>* Integrated design approach<br>* Interdisciplinary aspects<br>* Life cycle orientation | **Identify system feedback loops**<br>* Sensor(s)<br>* Control(s)<br>* Corrective action(s)<br>**Identify subsystem feedback loops**<br>* Sensor(s)<br>* Control(s)<br>* Corrective action(s)<br>**Identify informational aspects**<br>* Generation and control<br>* Life cycle orientation<br>**Identify technological aspects**<br>* Hardware<br>* Software<br>* Internal control<br>**Identify legitimate stakeholders**<br>* Internal<br>* External |

**Table 8.7**    Systems thinking supporting notes

| *Systems theory* | *Systems engineering* | *Cybernetics* |
| --- | --- | --- |
| **Purpose** | **Purpose** | **Purpose** |
| Systems theory elucidates the categorization context of the cost management system, aiding system designer(s) in comprehending its artificial, conceptual, and open-system attributes. It offers an initial understanding of the system's environment, input and output needs, and subsystem elements and connections. Additionally, it enhances the design framework and analytical approach at the system level | Systems engineering sets the system's application scope and domain, advancing to associated aspects, such as specifying requirements, understanding functional context, recognizing impacted disciplines and departments (including organizational ones), and contemplating the projected life cycle of system components | Cybernetics centers on aiding (sub)systems' objectives, emphasizing feedback mechanisms to attain those goals. This involves specifying inputs and establishing monitoring, management, and control approaches. It also encompasses recognizing informational and technological needs and identifying relevant stakeholders |
| **Additional aspects to consider** | **Additional aspects to consider** | **Additional aspects to consider** |
| * | * | * |
| * | * | * |
| * | * | * |

industry experts were assigned the fourth verification design statement (Table 8.12).

## 8.4    Reflection and Learning

This stage reflects the results of the verification and validation so far. Reflecting on the knowledge gained in the prior iterations, the current-iteration industry experts reiterated the significance of managerial costing systems for organizational value creation goals. Manufacturing settings are complex, having distinct processes, inputs, and outputs and challenging standardization. Recognizing this complexity, the experts affirmed the importance of designing effective managerial costing systems within this context. Thus, this iteration aimed to simplify and clarify supporting artifacts for the design process, easing complexity to some extent.

The industry experts agreed that successful organizational and performance management necessitates nuanced costing models beyond simple

**Table 8.8**  Cost accounting developmental guide

| Costing environment | Costing concepts | Cost accounting |
| --- | --- | --- |
| Define prevalent production environment | Define cost behavior characteristics | Define the appropriate costing approach |
| * Job costing | * Variable costs | * Absorption costing |
| * Process costing | * Fixed costs | * Marginal costing |
| * Operational costing | * Sticky costs | Define the appropriate costing method |
| Identify the operational departments | Consider aspects of controllability | * Standard costing |
| * Production departments | * Cost authority | * Operational costing: |
| * Support departments | * Direct cost classes | (1) GPK |
| | * Indirect cost classes | (2) ABC |
| | Consider aspects of planning | (3) RCA |
| | * Relevant costs | Identify related cost management concepts |
| | * Differential costs | * Theory of constraints |
| | * Opportunity costs | * Throughput accounting |
| | * Sunk costs | * Lean accounting |
| | | * Target costing |
| | | * Other |

ones reliant on external financial reporting systems for vital managerial choices. The core objective of the managerial costing system is to furnish internal cost data for informed decision-making. It must align with the organization's business environment to achieve this, incorporating operations, resources, and stakeholders. Interactions with the industry experts emphasized various crucial facets and considerations as follows:

- Risk entails potential adverse outcomes and involves the likelihood of facing unfavorable situations that may affect goals and resources. When initiating the design process, multiple risk categories should be examined. Examples include:

**Table 8.9**  Cost accounting supporting notes

| Costing environment | Costing concepts | Cost accounting |
|---|---|---|
| **Purpose** | **Purpose** | **Purpose** |
| The costing environment, often classified as job or process costing, clarifies the operational setting. Recognizing vital production and service departments and their connections is crucial despite potential hybrid concepts | Costing concepts underscore the vital importance of comprehending cost behavior. Equally, it is essential to bolster managerial understanding of cost control and planning implications across diverse cost categories | The cost accounting segment identifies and assesses relevant costing approaches and methods, considering operational realities and information requirements. Also, it ponders the potential impact and function of complementary concepts, such as the theory of constraints, throughput accounting, lean accounting, and target costing, in this framework |
| **Additional aspects to consider** | **Additional aspects to consider** | **Additional aspects to consider** |
| * | * | * |
| * | * | * |
| * | * | * |

- the risk of inadequate buy-in from critical stakeholders, spanning top management to operational and support functions; and
- the risk of inadequate buy-in from critical stakeholders, spanning top management to operational and support functions; and

• Causality involves the link between cause and effect, where one event or element (the cause) triggers another event or result (the effect). Aligning resources, activities, and products/services should create a logical structure that mirrors resource usage and operational aspects. This structure dramatically impacts cost allocation results more than individual drivers and their quantities do.

• Transparency involves honesty, clarity, and ease of understanding. It encompasses clear and accessible communication of information,

**Table 8.10** Business process developmental guide

| Business process definition | Business process management | Business process modeling |
|---|---|---|
| **Modeling: Define the primary purpose** | **Model abstraction** | **Functional decomposition requirements** |
| * Descriptive | * Vertical abstraction | * Value system |
| * Prescriptive | * Horizontal abstraction | * Value chain |
| * Explanatory | * Aggregate abstraction | * Business functions |
| **Modeling: Define the activity categories** | | * Business processes |
| * Manual activities | | **Identify the modeling notation approach** |
| * User-interaction activities | | * Swimlane |
| * System activities | | * UML |
| **Levels: Define the functional categories** | | * BPMN |
| * Core business functions | | * Other |
| * Critical support functions | | |
| * Peripheral functions | | |
| **Classification: Managerial functions** | | |
| * Strategic goals | | |
| * Business sustainability goals | | |
| **Classification: Operational functions** | | |
| * Interdepartmental functions | | |
| * Operational functions | | |
| * Automated functions | | |
| **Life cycle: Objectives** | | |
| * Analysis and design | | |
| * Modeling | | |
| * Implementation | | |
| * Monitoring | | |
| **Business improvement applications** | | |
| * Lean, JIT, TQM, Six Sigma | | |

**Table 8.11**  Business process supplementary notes

| Business process definition | Business process management | Business process modeling |
|---|---|---|
| **Purpose** | **Purpose** | **Purpose** |
| The business process definition sets the process model's purpose, considering process levels (core, critical support, peripheral), classification (managerial, operational), life cycle factors, and relevance of enhancement approaches such as lean, JIT, TQM, and Six Sigma | Business process management strives for targeted abstraction goals, spanning vertical, horizontal, and overall abstraction levels | Process modeling emphasizes practical modeling, analyzing the organization's value chain, business functions, and processes within the context of its value system. It then assesses and selects the suitable notation approach, whether actual or preferred |
| **Additional aspects to consider** | **Additional aspects to consider** | **Additional aspects to consider** |
| * | * | * |
| * | * | * |
| * | * | * |

**Table 8.12**  Fourth verification design statement

| | |
|---|---|
| **Design statement** | Project team members can understand and implement the process flow to meet crucial functional design prerequisites |
| **Response** | Consensus on *Strongly agree* (with a proviso) |
| **Notes** | Although there was general agreement that the integrated process flow complies with the design requirements, Some suggestions for improvement and clarification were given |
| | Concerning the process flow presentation, an iterative connection was proposed between *Cost behavior* and *Business functions* (indicated by the red arrow in Fig. 8.3). It was suggested that these may not be fully resolved before functional analysis owing to the complexity of cost behavior aspects, including managerial considerations. Hence, an iterative refinement process between these two activities is probable |
| | Based on participant feedback, additional explanatory notes were appended to the *multilevel dimensional costing process analysis* (indicated with underlining and italics in Table 8.13 |

procedures, and activities. Transparency boosts visibility and encourages openness. To gain acceptance, calculations across various cost allocation stages must be traceable.

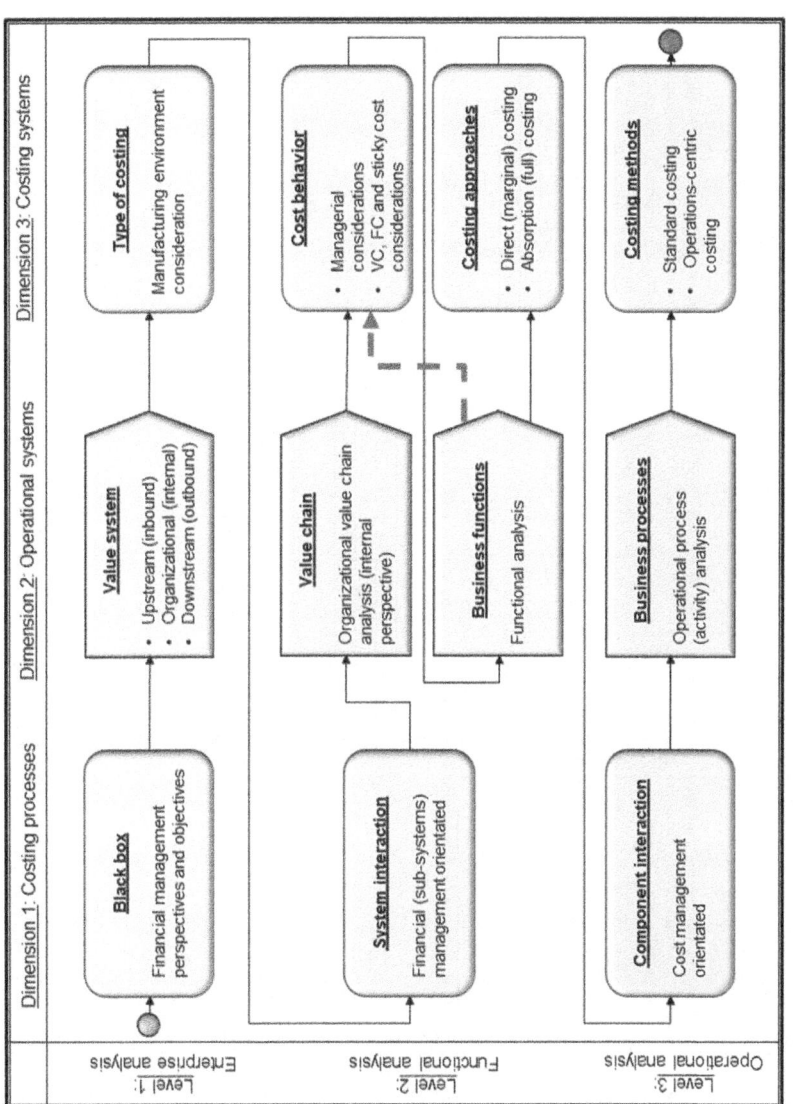

Fig. 8.3  Process flow for designing cost management systems

**Table 8.13**  Verified multilevel dimensional costing process analysis

**Level 1: Enterprise level:** Enterprise analysis focuses on high-level implications for effective cost management, emphasizing organizational impact rather than intricate costing methods

**Black box:** The foundational starting point of the process flow is a holistic reflection on the broader organizational value system. The focus should be on effective financial management and understanding the objectives of the managerial costing system in its specific scenario. This reflection aligns with the organization's strategies, mission, and vision, aiming to understand its role as both a consumer and generator of management information within the overall value system

*The organization's strategies, plans, and financial decisions should factor in the political, economic, socio-cultural, technological, legal, and environmental influences*

**Value system:** The process flow comes closer to the organization's business realities, and analyzing the organizational value stream is crucial for cost management initiatives. The value system considerations include (i) an inbound value stream analysis that considers external stakeholders, such as investors, financial resource providers, and suppliers, as their activities can impact the organization's costs, (ii) an internal value stream analysis as a high-level organizational analysis with a focus on sound financial management, and (iii) an outbound value stream analysis that focuses on external stakeholders that may influence the organization's financial and related cost management activities

*The inbound value stream analysis involves assessing business terms, contracts, and resource providers' dependability in supplying essential resources, which can influence production scheduling, product delivery, and cost management*

*The internal value stream analysis requires an understanding of how organizational actions impact the outbound value stream through inbound value stream traits. It is vital to align internal activities with inbound factors for a favorable outbound result*

**Type of costing:** The focus shifts to the operational production environment where the manufacturing activities take place. Before designing a sound managerial costing system, it is essential to clarify the basis of job, process, or operational (hybrid) costing in the context of the actual manufacturing environment. *This entails an understanding of the manufacturing setting, encompassing product type, production processes, and the intended customer*

*For the outbound value stream analysis, the organization first considers customers buying its products, focusing on their payment ability, sales terms, and credit provision, and determining selling prices through the cost management system. The organization then considers external consumers and report users impacted by the organization's financial performance, including periodic and regulatory reports."*

**Level 2: Functional level:** Functional analysis focuses on understanding the organizational system and related interactions

**(Sub)system interaction:** The focus is on the functions and interactions of financial subsystems. It is crucial to know which financial systems are in use (or should be) and to understand their capabilities. For analyzing the costing processes, it is vital that the various subsystems can relate and integrate seamlessly. Nevertheless, in the context of analyzing the costing processes, it is vital that the various subsystems can relate and integrate

*A robust general ledger system forms the base, possibly integrated into the organization's ERP systems Depending on management goals, extra finance modules might be needed. These can focus on operations such as inventory and payroll, not just financial reporting. Some ERP systems have cost management modules, but might not fit the organization's needs. In these cases, standalone or custom application software may be better*

**Value chain:** The initial second-level operational systems analysis centers on the organizational value chain, focusing on the functions of different business units from a cost management standpoint. It involves analyzing and understanding operational business functions considering Porter's *Value Chain Analysis*, and identifying primary production and secondary support departments

*Although functional analysis might match the hierarchical chart, it is crucial to have a profound understanding of operational roles and objectives*
**Business functions:** After understanding the cost behavior characteristics, the second iteration of operational analysis delves into a detailed functional analysis of activities within business functions. Another objective is identifying the most suitable basis and method for allocating the support departments' costs to the main production departments

**Cost behavior:** Once the high-level operational functions and interactions are understood, the initial costing systems investigation can begin. Within this context, the first key aspect is to clarify the management objectives of planning and control, which will also influence decisions regarding cost allocation approaches. A second analysis objective is to understand the cost behavior within the various functions, distinguishing between fixed costs, variable costs, and sticky costs. This understanding will directly impact later cost accounting activities, including clarifying production volumes for planning and cost allocation and allocating the basis of the support departments' costs

*This analysis can be closely linked with the subsequent business functions level, sometimes involving iterative steps*

(continued)

**Table 8.13** (continued)

| | | |
|---|---|---|
| | *The aim is to gain an understanding of the business functions within the value chain, not to delve into detailed process analysis. This is necessary in order to comprehend the organization's contextual informational needs* | **Costing approaches:** The choice between direct (marginal) and absorption (full) costing depends on the ultimate objective of the managerial costing system. Direct costing is the best option for supporting internal managerial decisions and achieving long-term value creation and economic viability objectives. However, if the managerial costing system needs to provide information for external reporting purposes, an absorption costing approach is seen as the appropriate choice |
| **Level 3: Operational level:** The operational analysis level focuses on practical cost management | | |
| **Component interaction:** In the last analysis level, the costing processes dimension involves understanding cost management and other related functions from a system components perspective. The focus is on identifying and analyzing specific requirements within the specific context, such as how cost information may need to be used in budgeting, planning, or supporting controlling activities | **Business processes:** In this operational analysis level, the focus is on actual process mapping (value stream mapping), involving selecting the most suitable process modeling application (for example, Swimlane, UML, or BPMN) based on the organization's user requirements and technological infrastructure capabilities, *taking into account user needs and technological capacity*<br><br>The purpose of mapping the business processes is to identify detailed activities, enabling the identification and possible elimination of nonvalue-adding activities and streamlining processes. This analysis should support the final selection and justification of the most appropriate costing method<br>*This analysis aids in choosing and justifying a suitable costing method* | **Costing methods:** Through completing the previous analyses, the organizational system has been well contextualized and understood, and the costing method is decided on. The configuration of the selected costing method then begins. *The configuration might demand specialized expertise, contingent on the organization's technological setup, design budget, and managerial needs* |

- Accountability involves taking responsibility for actions, decisions, and results and being answerable for behavior and performance. When assigning indirect costs (such as corporate overhead), it is vital to recognize that the control of operational management diminishes.
- Lastly, it was stressed that the managerial costing system should harmonize with the organization's values, value creation goals, resources, and operational cost relationships. Consequently, the process model should offer a principle-centric method for crafting a managerial costing system that supports decision-making without prescribing a specific costing approach.

## 8.5   Formalization of Learning

The conclusive step in the empirical phase is the formalization of learning. Throughout the book, supportive artifacts have been created, verified, and validated. This stage consolidates these efforts, formalizing the process model as a comprehensive artifact for facilitating the design of effective managerial costing systems.

As detailed throughout the process model's multidimensional design perspective connects integrated dimensions. Additionally, multilevel analysis builds upon aggregate-level analysis within the context of the *black box vs. subsystem interaction vs. component interaction analysis* concept, yielding a hierarchical model layout. In the final verification step, the industry experts were prompted to evaluate this within the framework of the fifth and final verification design statement, and the outcomes of this are shown in Table 8.14.

During the last process model validation activity, the industry experts were prompted to evaluate the above within the context of the second

**Table 8.14**   Fifth verification design statement

| | |
|---|---|
| **Design statement** | The process model should enable effective managerial costing systems design |
| **Response** | Consensus on *Strongly agree* |
| **Notes** | Since this cumulative model includes previously verified and validated components, it should enable the effective design of managerial costing systems |

**Table 8.15**    Second validation design statement

| | |
|---|---|
| **Design statement** | The integrated process model should aid in designing effective managerial costing systems |
| **Response** | Consensus on *Strongly agree* |
| **Notes** | As a comprehensive model encompassing various considerations, requirements, and stakeholders, the process model aims to enable the design of effective managerial costing systems. The industry experts, however, raised the question of whether the organizations would be prepared to undertake such an all-encompassing project. In this regard, two aspects noted were (i) the inherent commitment of resources required for such an endeavor and (ii) the need for a project team with the appropriate skill level to maximize the project's chances of success |

and final validation design statement. The outcomes of this are shown in Table 8.15.

Figure 8.4 offers an overview of the model arising from the interactions with and validation by the industry experts, supplemented by explanations of key objectives of each dimensional level.

The hierarchical layout depicted in the figure incorporates the previously validated developmental artifacts as its foundation. Aligning with the envisioned development methodology (from Chapter 2), the process model is the primary top-level representation, and auxiliary artifacts such as the supplementary guides and notes form the subsequent drill-down levels.

In conclusion, efficient managerial costing systems blend financial and operational data, providing new viewpoints on organizational performance. While these efforts might initiate from finance and emphasize financial matters, the system's sustainability depends on output demand. This demand is linked to the support and dedication of operational management, involving transparency, causality, and accountability. Recognizing this as a pivotal aspect of the cybernetic feedback loop is crucial.

## 8.6    Chapter Summary

This chapter aimed to validate the process model based on the research objective, building upon insights from the previous chapter. Verification and validation stemmed from the integrated three-dimensional concept, focusing on developmental artifacts from earlier iterations. The researcher–practitioner teams, including industry experts knowledgeable

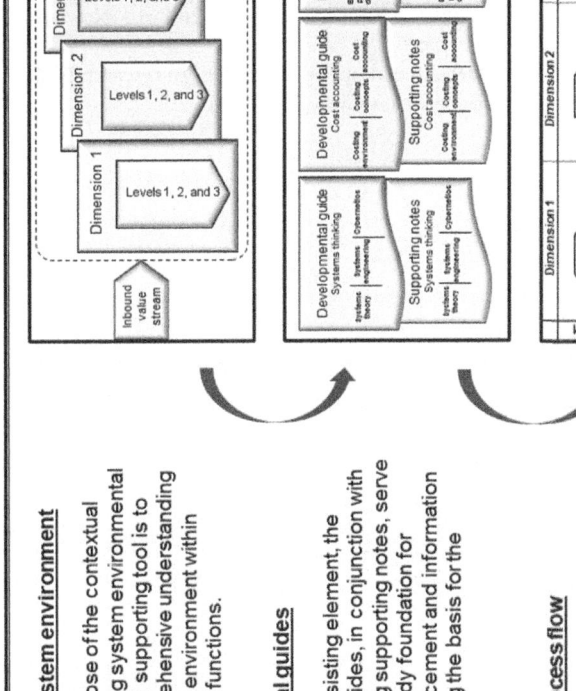

## 1. Contextual system environment

The primary purpose of the contextual managerial costing system environmental model as an initial supporting tool is to facilitate a comprehensive understanding of the operational environment within which the system functions.

## 2. Developmental guides

As the second assisting element, the developmental guides, in conjunction with the accompanying supporting notes, serve to establish a sturdy foundation for knowledge advancement and information gathering, forming the basis for the system's design.

## 3. Integrated process flow

Functioning as the ultimate supporting component, the integrated process flow leverages the aforementioned knowledge and information to steer the evolution of the managerial costing system methodically.

**Fig. 8.4**   Verified and validated process model

in managerial costing systems design and implementation, verified the design requirements and validated the intended outcomes. Suggestions for enhancement were integrated into the final model, which underwent formalization according to the ADR. The following chapter will offer a comprehensive discussion and conclusions for this research endeavor.

## References

Bryman, A. and Bell, E. 2007. *Business research methods*. 2nd ed. New York: Oxford University Press.

Mullarkey, M. and Hevner, A. 2019. An elaborated action design research process model. *European Journal of Information Systems*, 28(1):6–20.

# CHAPTER 9

# Summative Discussion

The previous chapter focused on the culmination of (i) the overall developmental process that embarked from a three-pillar literature basis and (ii) the empirical development process of the envisaged process model and the final verification and validation thereof. This final chapter serves as the concluding reflection on the practical application of the ADR approach and how it was applied in guiding the pragmatic solution to an actual business problem.

## 9.1 Introduction

The twenty-first-century manufacturing landscape is characterized by dynamic agility. The *Fourth Industrial Revolution* and emerging *Fifth Industrial Revolution* are giving rise to human–technology interactions previously seen only in science fiction, creating a pressure-filled, uncertain environment. Management faces immense pressure to achieve organizational value goals. Amidst this, effective resource management, especially cost management, is vital. The availability of pertinent information is crucial for effective management. Cost and management accounting aim to provide such information for sustainable resource use. The book's premise, supported by Maiyaki (2011) and Lawson et al. (2019), is that (i) proper managerial costing system commitment is lacking, despite the resource–product correlation, (ii) effective cost management must align

P. W. Buys, *Crafting Efficiency in Managerial Costing System Design*, https://doi.org/10.1007/978-981-97-0934-2_9

with operations, and (iii) cost management should quantitatively facilitate operational and resource management.

## 9.2    Reflection on Topic Actuality and Objectives

In the past, direct labor played a significant role in manufacturing costs, closely tied to indirect cost occurrence. This made direct labor costs a common choice for allocating indirect costs to products. However, owing to its diminishing significance in modern manufacturing and changing causality, it lost favor as a preferred allocation basis. Instead, operations-focused methods emerged to allocate indirect costs based on operational connections. This shift and the increase in technology-driven indirect costs and production support activities highlighted the need for cost structures that align with the intricate and swiftly changing production landscape. This realization emphasized the complexity of understanding managerial costing systems. Although managerial costing is often considered secondary to financial accounting, the primary aim of managerial costing systems is to estimate resource usage for informed decision-making. Thus, the problem reflected upon in the book is how to design an effective managerial costing system applicable to any manufacturing context.

The premise of the book is based on the following assumptions:

- The organization is viewed as a system with defined goals, components working together for synchronous goal attainment, and diverse stakeholders aligned with these goals.
- In contrast to rule-bound financial accounting, cost accounting and cost management allow for application that are more interpretive to support decision-making.

Analyzing business operations reveals interrelationships among subsystems and components within the organizational system. Modern operational improvement methods such as lean manufacturing, JIT, TQM, and Six Sigma emphasize the importance of optimized business operations, including effective cost management.

The ultimate goal was to ascertain whether a systems-based process modeling method could facilitate the creation of an effective managerial costing system. Three subgoals were set:

- Comprehending the intricate relationship between cost accounting and business processes within systems thinking frameworks.
- Devising a process modeling approach for crafting a managerial costing system that acknowledges organizational systems and their operational intricacies.
- Confirming the effectiveness of the process modeling approach in context.

The research structure was built around these subgoals, employing iterative steps using the eADR process. These will each be outlined and summarized in the following section.

## 9.3    ATTAINMENT OF THE RESEARCH OBJECTIVE

The following sub-sections provide some concluding reflections on the attainment of the book's objective, as formulated in Chapter 1. In the context of the design of effective cost management systems, some thoughts are focussed on the intricacies of systems thinking, cost accounting and business processes as the three pillars hereto, the process modeling approach to such system design and finally the validation of the modelling approach.

### 9.3.1    Systems Thinking, Cost Accounting and Business Processes Intricacies

A literature review found that, while managerial costing systems are vital for organizational value creation, several challenges hinder their effectiveness. Recognizing the vital role of business processes in selecting suitable cost accounting techniques and cost management practices is crucial for effective managerial costing systems. This necessitates adopting a systems thinking approach in organizational management. This forms the basis for the first subgoal: to comprehend the intricacies of and interaction between cost accounting and business processes within systems thinking context.

To achieve this goal, an extensive literature review of the three pillars was performed, and it revealed intricate complexities. As the first pillar, systems thinking encompassed the fundamentals of systems theory, a framework for conceptual systems design, engineering aspects, and cybernetics emphasizing stakeholder-oriented objectives. The second pillar, business processes addressed process concepts (modeling, levels, classification, life cycle, improvement), business process management, and process modeling techniques. As the final pillar, cost accounting, covered production environment insights, cost behavior, managerial goals, and various costing techniques.

The eADR iterations, particularly the initial problem-focused one, aimed to contextualize the research domain and refine the problem. In the first iteration, senior industry experts confirmed the significance of effective cost management, the underemphasis thereof in a system development context and the applicability of our proposed three-pillar approach. Collaborating with these experts, process flows for the three pillars were developed, resulting in sequential models that culminated in three developmental guides. These guides aid in collecting foundational information and requirements for subsequent system development. This diagnostic iteration formed the basis for the subsequent design iteration, which is discussed in the next section.

### 9.3.2    A Process Modeling Approach to Managerial Costing System Design

Subsequent to comprehending the intricate relationship between cost accounting and business processes within systems thinking frameworks, the second, object-centric, iteration aimed to shape the envisioned process model. The research problem was briefly revisited initially to reaffirm its complexity and validity. Cross-integration of the three pillars occurred during this phase, resulting in a three-dimensional understanding of the problem domain: costing processes, operational systems, and costing systems.

The researcher–practitioner team refined a multilevel process flow model during the BIE activities of this iteration. Beginning at the highest level, activities in the process flow consider enterprise-level aspects, encompassing a comprehensive contextual analysis of the organization's business environment within each dimension, before progressing to the next level. Afterward, the midlevel functional analysis focuses on a broader functional understanding within each dimension. Once sufficient functional insight has been gained, the process flow shifts to the final operational-level analysis across the three dimensions.

In terms of reflection and learning, the iteration concluded by establishing a model for the contextual environment of a managerial costing system. This framework is intended to visually represent the intricate setting in which an efficient managerial costing system operates. This design iteration set the stage for the validation activities in the subsequent iteration, which is elucidated in the next section.

### 9.3.3 Validating the Contextual Process Modeling Approach

The third iteration sought to validate the process model's relevance. A new cohort of industry experts experienced in managerial costing system design and implementation were involved in the verification and validation activities. These activities encompassed two main activities, namely verification and validation.

Firstly, in the context of *verification*, the supporting elements and the final process model were assessed against predetermined design criteria, yielding the following verified outcomes:

- The problem under consideration was validated as a pertinent and real-world business issue that could be alleviated through the design of effective cost management systems.
- Following minor technical enhancements, the contextual system environment model aids in aligning design team members' perspectives before the initiation of cost management system design.
- Despite potential limitations, the various developmental guides offer a valuable reference for collecting relevant data within the context.
- The resulting integrated process flow provides a coherent, step-by-step road map for guiding cost management system design endeavors.
- The overarching final process model, encompassing the aforementioned building blocks, can facilitate the creation of effective cost management systems.

Secondly, akin to the previous step, the following validated outcomes were obtained:

- The amalgamation of the three pillars (i.e., systems thinking, cost accounting, and business processes) into the three dimensions (i.e., costing processes, operational systems, and costing systems) constitutes a valid basis for understanding effective managerial costing systems.

- Serving as a comprehensive solution, the integrated process model is a valid developmental approach to the design of effective managerial costing systems.

## 9.4    CONCLUDING REFLECTION

In the quest for the ideal cost management approach and any debate over superior cost accounting techniques and their users, the consensus remains that effective cost management is all-encompassing and directly impacts organizational value creation. Unlike tightly regulated financial accounting, the application of cost and management accounting and its subdisciplines varies by organization, introducing two layers of complexity. Firstly, in cost and management accounting, numerous techniques (supportive and conflicting) exist, requiring organizations to choose the most suitable option, and secondly, this complexity is compounded by diverse organizational operations and stakeholder demands, necessitating an understanding of such intricacies.

Hence, the following question arises: Is the effort invested in crafting a comprehensive managerial costing system justified by its perceived benefits? This reality potentially accounts for organizations' hesitancy to embark or apprehension of embarking on the design of such a system. To address these concerns, a research approach rooted in the design science paradigm could offer a solution. Grounded in initial literature analysis, this book posited that viewing an organization as a system with multiple players, elements, and functions, along with the proposed three pillars, could bolster design of effective managerial costing systems. The eADR research iterations facilitated progressive investigation, allowing an interdisciplinary team to (i) examine a perceived business issue to confirm its industry relevance, (ii) devise a conceptual managerial costing system by integrating the foundational pillars into the dimensions of costing processes, operational systems, and costing systems, and (iii) conceptually validate that the resulting process model and managerial costing system environment model support effective design. Several artifacts were generated to address the research question: developmental guides for information collection, a model for contextualizing the managerial costing system environment, and a process model offering a logical road map for design.

It is vital to stress that the sophistication of managerial costing systems should align with the organization's environment, reflecting decision complexity and operational intricacy. Employing an ADR-based approach has demonstrated that a sequential, systems-oriented mindset can facilitate the design of effective managerial costing systems, demystifying the subject somewhat. However, the intricacy of organizational processes and cost accounting concepts persists. Although cost management efforts are often part of the general finance functions, designing effective systems demands (i) commitment from top management and resource allocation and (ii) operational function support (for example, manufacturing) to ensure practical implementation.

In addressing the research problem outlined in Chapter 1, the eADR approach demonstrated how integrating design science can help systematically develop effective managerial costing systems. This achieved both the primary objective and the subgoals. The proposed solution adheres to Hevner et al.'s (2004) validity criteria, as it creates a model (or method) for generating novel knowledge for a practical business issue, which includes verifying and validating its functionality and usability and showcasing tangible research contributions. The eADR process guarantees academic rigor via its design science foundation, aiming for an effective solution. Lastly, the researcher–practitioner team concept ensured relevant stakeholder communication.

## 9.5   Final Thoughts

Arguably, the main limitation of this research endeavor lies in its small participant sample. Five industry experts aided in the process model design and validation throughout the iterations. However, we did not seek to generalize industry findings but instead focused on design, creating an artifact to address a specific industry problem. The industry experts, being well versed in the issue, contributed their expertise to design and validate a process model (or methodology) to simplify the complexities of designing cost management systems.

This project concentrated on the initial three eADR iterations of process modeling, excluding the fourth iteration's evolutionary aspects. An opportunity for practical implementation of this project would arise should an organization seek to design its own managerial costing system

This, however, could demand substantial resource commitment in terms of human, financial, and technological resources. Furthermore, such a project might be adaptable to various technological and manufacturing settings, such as exploring specific job costing versus process costing scenarios or high-tech versus low-tech environments within manufacturing. It may also evolve into industries beyond manufacturing, such as diverse service-related contexts, including financial services, consulting, healthcare, and academia.

## References

Hevner, A.R., March, S.T. and Park, J. 2004. Design science in information systems research. *MIS Quarterly*, 28(1): 75–105.

Lawson, R., Cokins, G., Hicks, D.T., Krumwiede, K., Swain, M.R. and White, L.R. 2019. Developing an effective managerial costing model. Statements on Management Accounting. Institute of Management Accountants (IMA), Montvale, N.J.

Maiyaki, A.A. 2011. The practicability of activity-based costing (ABC) in the Nigerian Retail Bank. *Business Intelligence Journal*, 4(2):351-354.

# Index

**A**

Action design research (ADR), 22,
23, 25, 30, 107–110, 122, 123,
131, 133, 134, 143, 147, 149,
150, 170, 171, 177
Action research (AR), 19, 21, 22
Activity-based costing (ABC), 95,
97–99, 102, 129, 137, 159


**B**

Business processes, 1, 4, 5, 7, 9, 12,
19, 49, 53–58, 61–65, 69, 70,
77, 107, 111, 112, 115, 118,
122, 123, 125, 127, 128,
135–137, 142, 143, 152, 154,
161, 166, 173–175
Business process management (BPM),
4, 5, 53, 58, 62, 63, 65, 70,
123, 127, 161, 162, 174
Business process reengineering (BPR),
60, 62, 63, 70

**C**

Cost accounting, 2–7, 9, 12, 19, 57,
72, 77, 90, 95, 96, 102, 107,
111, 114, 120–123, 125, 128,
129, 135–138, 141, 143, 152,
154, 159, 160, 165, 172–177

Cost behavior, 81–83, 89, 99, 102,
120, 138, 141, 159, 160, 162,
165, 174

Costing processes, 133, 135–138,
141, 142, 144, 152, 154, 165,
166, 174, 176

Costing systems, 12, 39, 56, 72, 78,
83, 91, 94, 99, 103, 111, 113,
114, 116, 122, 123, 133–135,
137, 138, 141, 143, 144,
149–155, 159, 164–167,
171–177

Cost management, 1–7, 9, 12, 13,
19, 27, 28, 30, 38, 40, 44, 47,
49, 54–57, 77, 81, 84, 85, 89,
91, 92, 95, 97, 101, 109,
111–115, 122, 129, 132,

135–137, 140–142, 152–154, 158, 159, 163–166, 171–177
Cybernetics, 33, 43, 44, 46, 47, 49, 55, 118, 124, 126, 157, 158, 173

**D**

Design science, 2, 7, 8, 12, 13, 18, 19, 21, 22, 26, 28, 30, 176, 177
Design science research (DSR), 21, 22
Developmental guides, 110, 123–129, 148, 149, 151, 153, 155–157, 159, 161, 174–176

**E**

eADR iteration, 30, 103, 108, 143, 153, 174, 177
Elaborated action design research (eADR), 10, 22, 25, 26, 30, 43, 107, 116, 123, 131, 143, 148, 173, 176, 177

**I**

Industrial revolution, 5

**L**

Lean accounting, 101, 102, 120, 129, 159, 160
Lean manufacturing, 3, 6, 60, 61, 127, 172

**M**

Management cybernetics, 12, 46, 47
Managerial costing system, 1–3, 5–9, 12, 13, 17–19, 21, 26–28, 30, 34–40, 42–44, 47, 49, 53, 55, 56, 58, 62, 63, 65, 67, 70, 81, 85, 95, 97, 99, 102, 107, 111,

113–116, 122, 123, 125, 131–133, 135, 137, 138, 140, 141, 143, 145, 147, 149, 151–156, 158, 164, 167, 168, 170, 172, 173, 175–177
Manufacturing, 1, 2, 5–8, 11, 12, 17, 27, 28, 40, 41, 60–62, 78, 79, 85, 86, 91, 97, 107, 109, 111, 136, 138, 140, 143, 151, 152, 164, 171, 172, 177, 178

**O**

Operational systems, 135, 137, 138, 141, 143, 144, 151–153, 155, 165, 174, 176
Organizational systems, 6, 7, 34, 37, 40, 124, 131, 135, 137, 138, 140, 142, 143, 156, 157, 165, 166, 172, 173

**P**

Process flow, 11, 12, 109, 116–122, 125, 131, 133, 138–140, 144, 148, 149, 151, 153, 155, 156, 162–164, 174, 175
Process improvement, 54, 60, 62, 65, 127
Process model, 4, 7, 9, 13, 28, 29, 36, 53–55, 59, 60, 63–65, 67, 70, 71, 78, 103, 118, 122, 127, 133, 143–145, 147, 150, 151, 153, 154, 156, 162, 167–169, 171, 174–177

**S**

Six Sigma, 61, 62, 118, 127, 161, 162, 172
Stakeholders, 3, 7, 23, 29, 30, 34–36, 42, 44, 46–49, 54, 55, 58, 59, 68, 69, 85, 112, 114–116, 118,

122, 126, 127, 135, 136, 140,
143, 153, 154, 157–160, 164,
168, 172, 173, 176, 177

Systems engineering, 12, 33, 40–43,
49, 118

Systems environment, 11, 36

Systems theory, 3, 4, 9, 12, 19, 20,
33, 34, 43, 49, 116, 124, 157,
158, 173

Systems thinking, 4, 7, 9, 12, 19, 33,
34, 43, 44, 46, 49, 53, 55, 107,
111, 113–116, 120, 122, 123,
125, 133, 135, 137, 149, 151,
152, 154, 156–158, 173–175

**T**
Target costing, 102, 120, 129, 138,
159, 160
Theory of constraints, 101, 102, 120,
129, 159, 160
Throughput accounting, 101, 102,
120, 129, 143, 159, 160
Total quality management (TQM), 6,
61, 62, 118, 127, 161, 162, 172

**V**
Value chain, 4, 28, 61, 65, 66, 79,
113, 120, 128, 137, 141, 161,
162, 165
Value system, 37, 66, 70, 120, 128,
137, 140, 161, 162, 164

The manufacturer's authorised representative in the EU is Springer
Nature Customer Service Centre GmbH, Europaplatz 3, 69115 Heidelberg,
Germany. If you have any concerns regarding our products, please
contact ProductSafety@springernature.com

Printed and bound by CPI Group (UK) Ltd, Croydon, CR0 4YY
27/04/2026
02097562-0002